I Arise Today

A 40 Day Journey through St. Patrick's Breastplate Prayer

Craig J. Sefa

Copyright 2019 by Craig J. Sefa
All rights reserved.
ISBN: 9781701189836

Unless otherwise noted, Scripture quotations are taken from the New Revised Standard Version Bible, copyright © 1989 the Division of Christian Education of the National Council of the Churches of Christ in the United States of America. Used by permission. All rights reserved.

Scripture quotations marked NIV are taken from the Holy Bible, New International Version®, NIV® Copyright ©1973, 1978, 1984, 2011 by Biblica, Inc.® Used by permission. All rights reserved worldwide.

Scripture quotations marked MSG are taken from THE MESSAGE, copyright © 1993, 2002, 2018 by Eugene H. Peterson. Used by permission of NavPress. All rights reserved. Represented by Tyndale House Publishers, Inc.

Cover Photo by Craig J. Sefa, "Croagh Patrick", County Mayo, Ireland, 2016.

DEDICATION

to Gram…

The stories we made up together when I was a child
sparked my desire to write from before I can remember.

Your ongoing example of devoted prayer and faith
throughout my life has truly been an inspiration.

Your love and prayers
mean more than you will ever know.

CONTENTS

	Acknowledgments	ix
	St. Patrick's Breastplate Prayer	1
	Introduction	5
Day 01	I Arise Today	10
Day 02	Three – One Creator	14
Day 03	Birth & Baptism	18
Day 04	Crucifixion & Burial	22
Day 05	Resurrection & Ascension	27
Day 06	Judgment of Doom	31
Day 07	Angels & Archangels	35
Day 08	Resurrection & Reward	40
Day 09	Saints	44
Day 10	Heaven	49
Day 11	Sun	54
Day 12	Moon	59
Day 13	Fire	63
Day 14	Lightning	67

Day 15	Wind	72
Day 16	Sea	77
Day 17	Earth	82
Day 18	Rock	87
Day 19	Pilot	92
Day 20	Might	97
Day 21	Wisdom	102
Day 22	God's Eye	108
Day 23	God's Ear	113
Day 24	God's Word	119
Day 25	God's Hand	124
Day 26	God's Shield	129
Day 27	God's Host	133
Day 28	Snares of Devils	138
Day 29	Temptation of Vices	143
Day 30	Everyone who shall wish me ill	147
Day 31	I Summon Today	151
Day 32	Against every knowledge that corrupts	155

Day 33	Poison, Burning, Drowning, Wounding	160
Day 34	Christ with me	166
Day 35	Christ before me, Christ behind me	172
Day 36	Christ in me	177
Day 37	Christ beneath me, Christ above me	181
Day 38	Christ on my right, Christ on my left	186
Day 39	Christ when I lie down, Christ when I sit down, Christ when I arise	191
Day 40	Christ in Everyone	196
Day 41	On Endings as New Beginnings	201
	A Celtic Blessing	205

ACKNOWLEDGMENTS

Thank you to Dr. Reginald Johnson
for serving as my teacher, mentor and spiritual
director at Asbury Theological Seminary.

You inspired my interest in Celtic Christianity
and led the spiritual pilgrimage to Ireland
where we prayed the prayer of St. Patrick every day.

I promised myself on that trip that I would unpack the richness of this prayer. This is the fruit of that commitment.

ST. PATRICK'S BREASTPLATE PRAYER

I invite you to pray along with me on video at
www.craigsefa.org/arise/resources

I arise today
Through a mighty strength, the invocation of the Trinity,
Through belief in the Threeness,
Through confession of the Oneness
   of the Creator of creation.

I arise today
Through the strength of Christ's birth with His baptism,
Through the strength of His crucifixion with His burial,
Through the strength of His resurrection
   with His ascension,
Through the strength of His descent
   for the judgment of doom.

I arise today
Through the strength of the love of cherubim,
In the obedience of angels,
In the service of archangels,
In the hope of resurrection to meet with reward,
In the prayers of patriarchs,
In the predictions of prophets,
In the preaching of apostles,

In the faith of confessors,
In the innocence of holy virgins,
In the deeds of righteous men.

I arise today, through
The strength of heaven,
The light of the sun,
The radiance of the moon,
The splendor of fire,
The speed of lightning,
The swiftness of wind,
The depth of the sea,
The stability of the earth,
The firmness of rock.

I arise today, through
God's strength to pilot me,
God's might to uphold me,
God's wisdom to guide me,
God's eye to look before me,
God's ear to hear me,
God's word to speak for me,
God's hand to guard me,
God's shield to protect me,
God's host to save me
From snares of devils,
From temptation of vices,
From everyone who shall wish me ill,
   afar and near.

I summon today
All these powers between me and those evils,
Against every cruel and merciless power
that may oppose my body and soul,
Against incantations of false prophets,

Against black laws of pagandom,
Against false laws of heretics,
Against craft of idolatry,
Against spells of witches and smiths and wizards,
Against every knowledge that corrupts
   man's body and soul;

Christ to shield me today
Against poison, against burning,
Against drowning, against wounding,
So that there may come to me an abundance of reward.

Christ with me,
Christ before me,
Christ behind me,
Christ in me,
Christ beneath me,
Christ above me,
Christ on my right,
Christ on my left,
Christ when I lie down,
Christ when I sit down,
Christ when I arise,

Christ in the heart of everyone who thinks of me,
Christ in the mouth of everyone who speaks of me,
Christ in every eye that sees me,
Christ in every ear that hears me.

I arise today
Through a mighty strength, the invocation of the Trinity,
Through belief in the Threeness,
Through confession of the Oneness
   of the Creator of creation. Amen.

INTRODUCTION

40 DAYS ON PATRICK'S MOUNTAIN

Tuesday, June 21st, 2016 –

I boarded a plane for a 10-day spiritual pilgrimage through Ireland with my spiritual director from seminary, Dr. Reg Johnson, along with a group of other Asbury Seminary Alumni. My heart has long been stirred by the art, music, and rich spiritual traditions from this "Land of Saints and Scholars" and the early Celtic Saints, though I knew very little about them before this pilgrimage.

One month before my trip, I wrote the following entry in my journal:

> When Jesus turned and saw them following, he said to them, *"What are you looking for?"* They said to him, "Rabbi" (which translated means Teacher), *"where are you staying?"* He said to them, *"Come and see."* (John 1:38-39a)
>
> I cannot fully understand the echoes of Celtic Christianity that resonate within me, yet I hear their call all the same. In truth, I know very little about these mystical saints of old. The intricate detail of Celtic art, the beauty of Celtic music and the Irish landscape, and the mystery of their intimacy with the Holy inspire me to draw near… to learn… and to know my Creator more deeply than I have ever known.
>
> "Rabbi, where are you staying?" I ask.
>
> I know he stays in my church, my home, my Bible, my heart… indeed the Risen Christ is present everywhere I turn. But these places are noisy, cluttered, and distorted by modern cultural lenses and the blur of everyday routine.
>
> Once upon a time, the Rabbi stayed on the quiet green

hills of Ireland while the rest of the world struggled through war and darkness. It was said to be a haven for saints and scholars who as Thomas Cahill puts it, would later save all western civilization.[1] In this season I prepare to go to this ancient, quiet, and sacred place... a Thin Place... in search of a fresh awakening of God's Holy Presence within me.

I still know very little about the great Irish saints. It is difficult to truly know them, at least in part because we have so little written record of their lives and ministries. The limited sources we do have tend to blur historical facts with myths and legends. I find the legends of the saints fascinating as they reflect the miraculous, larger than life impact these Godly men and women had on the ancient people of Ireland.

Every day in Ireland we prayed portions of St. Patrick's Breastplate Prayer, or "The Lorica of St. Patrick." It is a prayer not for direction or answers, at least not to the kinds of questions I was asking about God's next steps for my life. Rather, this is a prayer of "being," a way of being fully present with God and surrendering in full reliance on God each day, no matter where the path may lead.

Before coming home, I vowed I would spend time

---

[1] Thomas Cahill, *How the Irish Saved Civilization: The Untold Story of Ireland's Heroic Role from the Fall of the Rome to the Rise of Medieval Europe*, 1995.

drinking deeply from the sacred well of this prayer. As it happens, life took over and my great intentions quickly faded.

In January 2019, I finally committed to a one-year journey through the Breastplate Prayer of St. Patrick using my blog as a means of personal accountability. As I began laying out the lines and stanzas of the prayer on the calendar, I was surprised to find that it fit nicely into 40 days. While many people use 40-day devotionals for Lent, I invite you to join me in this prayer any time of year. 40 days with St. Patrick's prayer might offer a perfect beginning for a new year or perhaps a season of reflection and self-examination in the fall as the year comes to an end. Whenever you choose to use these reflections, I pray God will richly bless your journey.

The idea of a 40-day devotional cemented even further when I thought about the life of St. Patrick.[2] Croagh Patrick or "Patrick's Mountain" remains one of my favorite places in Ireland. On this mountain it is said that St. Patrick fasted and prayed for 40 days, after which he cast all the snakes out of Ireland.

---

[2] St. Patrick's Breastplate prayer, though commonly attributed to St. Patrick, was likely not written by the great saint of Ireland. Nevertheless, the ideas throughout this prayer reflect the life and teachings of St. Patrick.

Now there were never any real snakes in Ireland, but his 40-day fast on the mountain helped prepare Patrick to bring Christianity to what much of the Western world viewed as a God-forsaken island of pagans. St. Patrick's mission to "drive all the snakes out of Ireland" has quite literally become the stuff of legend. I believe the spirit of St. Patrick's Breastplate prayer reflects the kinds of prayers Patrick must have prayed upon this mountain and throughout his life as he risked everything to proclaim the Good News of salvation to the very people who had once enslaved him as a boy.[3]

And so, I invite you to join me for the next 40 days on St. Patrick's Mountain, just as Christ prayed for 40 days in the wilderness. Such 40-day journeys often mark seasons of preparation. Preparation for what? We may not yet know. But I believe God honors such devotion and by the time you are ready to come down from this mountain, my prayer is that God's call for the next season of your life and mission in the world will become clearer.

Throughout this journey and beyond, may you arise each day in the mighty strength of the Three-One God, "driving out the snakes" along your path wherever the Spirit may lead.

---

[3] J. M Holmes, *The Real Saint Patrick* (Ballyclare, Antrim: Irish Hill Publications, 2002).

DAY 01

I ARISE TODAY

*I arise today,
through a mighty strength,
the invocation of the Trinity…*

Welcome to the first step of our 40-day journey through St. Patrick's Breastplate Prayer.

Beginning with the refrain, "I arise today," we are invited to follow the leading of the Apostle Paul when he calls us to "put on the whole armor of God" (Ephesians 6:10-18). We call upon the Triune God as our source of strength for every moment of every day and we reflect on the numerous means God uses to shield us and guide us as we seek to live faithfully in the midst of evil and temptation.

Other versions of this prayer say: "I bind unto myself today…" I am reminded of Paul's words to the Colossians:

> As God's chosen ones, holy and beloved, clothe yourselves with compassion, kindness, humility, meekness, and patience. Bear with one another and, if anyone has a complaint against another, forgive each other; just as the Lord has forgiven you, so you also must forgive. Above all, clothe yourselves with love, which binds everything together in perfect harmony (Colossians 3:12-14).

"Binding unto ourselves" the Three-One God is much like putting on the love of Christ which "binds everything together in perfect harmony." When we arise each day, we put on the clothing appropriate for the tasks we face. We may put on a uniform, a suit, a set of work-out clothes or even a comfortable pair of jeans or sweats. Just as our clothing is specific to the activities of our day, so arising each day and "binding God unto ourselves" provides us with everything we need for the day ahead.

We talk a great deal in the Western church about "believing in God," which often translates to little more than accepting the reality of God's existence. In terms of salvation we might expand that belief to accepting the truth of Jesus' divine nature, his death and resurrection, and the forgiveness of sins through grace.

While belief and knowledge are vital to our faith, following Jesus is more about a way of being than a way of thinking. It is about being perfected in love and this requires not merely that we gain more knowledge or greater achievements, but that we learn to live in peace with God, with one another, and even with ourselves. It is about arising each day in the Three-One God and putting on Christ so that Christ lives through us.

As we begin this journey together, may we seek to "arise each day" with the Light of Christ upon our paths, to "bind unto ourselves" each day the gifts and the power of the Holy Spirit, and to become ever more dependent on the strength and love of the Mighty Three-One God.

Reflections:

What do you think about the statement, "Following Jesus is more about a way of being than a way of thinking?"

What is your first instinct when you arise each day? What is the first thought that comes to your mind?

How might your day look different if you began by calling upon the mighty strength of God?

DAY 02

THREE – ONE CREATOR

> I arise today,
> Through belief in the Threeness,
> Through confession of the Oneness,
> of the Creator of creation

Why does the Trinity matter?

Many people call upon the strength of God, or at least some higher spiritual power. Yet Christians insist on complicating the identity of God with the inconceivable doctrine of the Trinity; three persons, yet one God. Are we simply trying to be obtuse and exclusive, or does this three-ness and oneness truly make a difference?

I find it interesting that of all the religions in our world, only three insist there is only One God; Judaism, Christianity, and Islam. All three, though often embroiled in fierce war without and within, claim the same source; the self-revelation of the God of Abraham, Isaac and Jacob.

The very existence of even one, let alone three, long-standing monotheistic religions amid an endless spiritual smorgasbord speaks volumes about the truth of this one God and Creator of creation. In a world where people can worship or not worship anything or nothing, why would anyone conceive of monotheism in the first place? Such single-minded worship would have been absurd and unthinkable. No one in the ancient world could have imagined that there might only be one God, unless of course this one and only God reached out to a feeble and limited human being like Abraham who had just the slightest inclination to believe the impossible (Genesis 12:1-9).

God, by definition, must be self-sufficient. Therefore, God did not need to create. God certainly did not need to create or "give birth to" such selfish free-willed beings who would do so much harm to one another and all of creation.

That's where the Three-ness and Oneness thing comes into play. If God's very nature is Triune, then God did not exist from all eternity as an isolated, independent being.

Rather, God's very nature is relational. This is what it means to say that "God is Love" (1 John 4:8).

How can there be love apart from relationship? Relationship with humanity, sure; but what about God as Love before humans took their first breath? God is, was, and always will be love, with or without created beings. Therefore, God must be a relational being, existing in an eternal dance between Father, Son & Spirit.

In this case, God's nature compelled the creation of free-willed beings in the same way that our relational nature compels us, even the most isolated and independent among us, to long for some form of connection with others. Our desire to be known and to be loved is as inherent as our need for food or water. The same is true with God; Father, Son, and Spirit in eternal relationship; love freely chosen from everlasting to everlasting. This is the very nature of God. Apart from relationship, God would no longer be Love. God could no longer be God.

Whether in a day or over a thousand years, God created human beings in the Divine Image, to love and to be loved and to share in the eternal joy that is the Three-ness and the Oneness of the Creator of creation.

Reflections:

In what ways have you encountered or experienced the relational nature of God?

How might the three-ness and the oneness of God affect the way you pray?

Considering the nature of the Trinity, what does it mean to you that *you* are created in the Image of this three-one God?

DAY 03

BIRTH & BAPTISM

*I arise today
through the strength
of Christ's birth with His baptism*

We talk a great deal about the birth and baptism of Christ in the early weeks of each new year. Both events mark significant moments of Jesus' life and ministry. They teach us what it means that God took on flesh and dwelt among us.

Yet with the endless array of theological sermons I could preach on these two events, I'm not sure I've ever associated the word "strength" with either. Nor, I confess, have I given much thought to how these two historical moments of Jesus' life might impact my rising each day.

We generally associate birth and baptism with the weakness and innocence of children. Some say that our mothers should be the ones to receive gifts on our birthdays because they did all the work to bring us into the world. They don't call it "labor" for nothing.

Likewise, in baptism we take a more passive role. When an infant or child is baptized, parents and congregations take vows to raise that child in the faith. Even as believers who choose to be baptized, we still take on a submissive role by allowing ourselves to be "buried with Christ" so that Christ may raise us up to walk in a new life (Romans 6:4).

This strength in which we arise each day is not only the strength of our own birth and baptism, but of Christ's. For Jesus, both events are primarily about his identity.

> And now, you will conceive in your womb and bear a son, and you will name him Jesus. He will be great, and will be called the Son of the Most High (Luke 1:31-32a).

> And when Jesus had been baptized, just as he came up from the water, suddenly the heavens were opened to him and he saw the Spirit of God descending like a

dove and alighting on him. And a voice from heaven said, "This is my Son, the Beloved, with whom I am well pleased" (Matthew 3:16-17).

In Christ's birth and baptism, Jesus is affirmed and reaffirmed as the Son of God. Through our new birth in Christ and by the grace of God poured out upon us in baptism, we are adopted as sons and daughters of God.

See what love the Father has given us, that we should be called children of God; and that is what we are (1 John 3:1a).

To arise in the strength of Christ's birth and baptism is to arise in the strength of our true identity in Christ. We are sons and daughters of the Most High God.

Reflections:

When you look in the mirror, can you truly see a son or daughter of God? Why or why not?

What strength might you find today by claiming your identity in Christ?

As you go through your daily routine, how might others notice the presence of Christ in you?

DAY 04

CRUCIFIXION & BURIAL

*I arise today
through the strength
of His crucifixion with His burial*

"I arise today through the strength..."

As we stretch our arms and set our feet on the floor, we take a deep breath and inhale the strength of Almighty God for the day ahead.

But this strength seems to come from strange places. Yesterday our strength came from the birth and baptism of Christ… both passive acts that we do not generally associate with strength.

Today our strength comes from crucifixion and burial.

With every fiber of our being we want to keep going with the liturgy. Like a melody that ends on a suspended chord, we desperately want to jump to the resolution. After all, we know the great mystery of faith:

> Christ has died.
>
> Christ is risen.
>
> Christ will come again!

But the disciples did not arise on Saturday morning in the strength of resurrection. They arose to the reality of death. I imagine like us, strength was not the first thing they felt in the face of the overwhelming darkness of their reality.

Perhaps we should pause this week and ask what strength we might find in the crucifixion and burial of Christ. We do not consider this as though the resurrection never happened, for as the apostle Paul writes,

> If Christ has not been raised, your faith is futile, and you are still in your sins (1 Corinthians 15:17).

Rather, we pause to experience the full weight and power of death, of pain, of sorrow, of grief, of fear, just as the disciples felt on Saturday morning.

The power and apparent finality of death can paralyze even the strongest and most joyful person. We typically avoid thinking about our own mortality at all cost. We don't want to wake up to the idea that this day could be our last.

We face death every day of our lives. People we know and love are dying. We are dying. As a doctor once told a cancer patient, "We are all born with a terminal illness. It's called life."

More than that, we are called to take up our cross, to be crucified with Christ, and to be buried with him through baptism into death (Romans 6:4). Every sacrifice we make for the sake of others or for the sake of the gospel requires a little death inside of us.

There is great strength in willingly taking up our cross (Matthew 16:24-25).

There is great strength required to pray like Jesus for the forgiveness of the very people who have nailed us to the tree (Luke 23:34).

There is great strength in the knowledge that we can "rest in peace" even before we take our last breath (John 4:14, 1 John 5:11).

Only when death loses its sting and the fear of death holds no power over us can we truly experience the freedom to live (1 Corinthians 15:55).

Reflections:

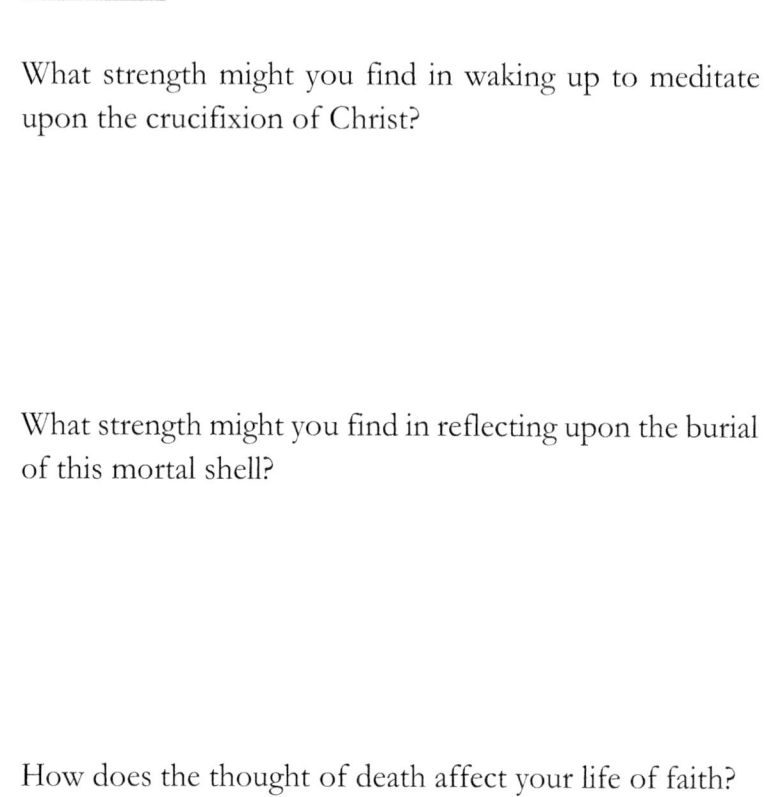

What strength might you find in waking up to meditate upon the crucifixion of Christ?

What strength might you find in reflecting upon the burial of this mortal shell?

How does the thought of death affect your life of faith?

DAY 05

RESURRECTION & ASCENSION

*I arise today
through the strength
of His resurrection with His ascension*

Resurrection!

Now that's the kind of strength we've been waiting for. We struggled yesterday to find strength in death when what we truly long for is the power over death.

I sometimes imagine the conflicting emotions the disciples must have felt. They knew Jesus had power over death. He raised Lazarus (John 11:38-44). He raised

Jairus' daughter (Mark 5:21-43). But Jesus was alive when he performed those incredible miracles. If Jesus is in the grave, how can he raise himself?

Yet even this is easily within God's power. As Fredrick Buechner says, **resurrection reminds us that the worst thing is never the last thing.**[4] The hope of resurrection gives us the strength to face the worst things.

What about strength in Christ's ascension?

We're not talking about the strength to fly, or even to be "caught up in the sky" with Jesus as some describe the last days. We're talking about finding our strength in Jesus' ascension. This is a bit more difficult because in some ways we wish he had never left.

Wouldn't the church and the Kingdom be stronger if Jesus had stayed on earth to run things himself instead of trusting his followers to keep it all straight for a few thousand years?

Where do we find strength in the ascension?

At first glance, I find at least one key strength in the ascension through the coming of the Holy Spirit.

---

[4] Fredrick Buechner referenced in "The Worst Thing Is Not the Last Thing," Adam Hamilton, accessed November 6, 2019, https://www.adamhamilton.com/blog/the-worst-thing-is-not-the-last-thing.

Nevertheless I tell you the truth: it is to your advantage that I go away, for if I do not go away, the Advocate will not come to you; but if I go, I will send him to you (John 16:7).

I often ask the question, "If you could spend just one hour in person with Jesus or a lifetime with the Holy Spirit, which would you choose?"

Who wouldn't jump at a chance to meet face to face with Jesus? We tend to get stuck in a spiritual holding pattern waiting to land in heaven where Jesus will meet us at the gate, because of course there is no TSA in heaven instructing him to wait in the baggage claim.

Jesus chose to limit himself to time and space so that we could know God, but Holy Spirit has no such limitation.

Holy Spirit is just as much the real presence of God as Jesus in the flesh; only where Jesus dwelt *among* us, the Spirit dwells *within* us. We don't have to make an appointment or struggle to lower our problems through the roof of some poor soul's home to get an audience with God (Mark 2:1-12).

We call upon the strength of the resurrection but let us not wait until we are raised to live in that strength. The strength of the ascension is available now as the Holy Spirit prays on our behalf for all we need (Romans 8:26).

Reflections:

Do you ever feel like the strength of the resurrection is a future, after-death kind of reality?

In what ways do you find strength in the ascension of Christ?

Would you rather spend an hour with Jesus or a lifetime with the Holy Spirit (on this side of eternity)? Why?

DAY 06

JUDGMENT OF DOOM

> I arise today
> through the strength
> of His descent for the judgment of doom

Judgement of Doom?

That's not something we pray very often, if ever.

One caveat before I dig into my own reflections.

Some ideas in this prayer comes from Patrick's Catholic tradition. As a protestant, though I grew up Catholic, I am not explicitly familiar with all the nuanced meanings of this theology. I seek only to help guide our mediation as we pray this ancient and sacred prayer together.

That being said, let's get back to today's "strength": the strength of His descent for the judgement of doom. I cannot even type that line without hearing C3PO's voice from Star Wars declaring, "We're doomed!"[5]

Let us consider one of the most common scriptures used to affirm this idea of Christ's descent into Hades.

> For Christ also suffered for sins once for all, the righteous for the unrighteous, in order to bring you to God. He was put to death in the flesh, but made alive in the spirit, *in which also he went and made a proclamation to the spirits in prison*, who in former times did not obey, when God waited patiently in the days of Noah, during the building of the ark, in which a few, that is, eight persons, were saved through water (1 Peter 3:18-20).

Whether this text refers to a literal descent into hell may be debated among scholars for centuries to come. It seems, however, that between Christ's burial and his resurrection, he did not simply exist as a lifeless corpse like a princess waiting to be awoken by true love's kiss. Regardless of whether we are talking about a literal "hell"

---

[5] George Lucas, *Star Wars Episode IV: A New Hope* (20th Century Fox, 1977). Just for fun, you can find the video link at craigsefa.org/arise/resources. Day 6.

or not, Jesus fully descended into death, Hades, the spirit-world, or whatever else we might call it.

According to Peter, Jesus proclaimed the good news of hope to those in prison there. In some way, captives were released (Ephesians 4:8). It remains unclear who these captives included or what their "prison" entailed, but we do see the dead being raised after Jesus was crucified.

> The tombs also were opened, and many bodies of the saints who had fallen asleep were raised. After his resurrection they came out of the tombs and entered the holy city and appeared to many (Matthew 27:52-53).

Doom may simply be defined as "death". Whatever Jesus did between taking his last breath on the cross and stepping out of the tomb, we can be certain of this: he declared one final and absolute judgement against death and "doom."

> "Death has been swallowed up in victory."
> "Where, O death, is your victory?"
> "Where, O death, is your sting?" (1 Corinthians 15:55)

Let us arise today in the strength of Christ's victory of death and His final judgement of doom.

Reflections:

What do you think about the idea that the strength of Christ is present and active during those three days between his death and resurrection?

What does the "judgement of doom" mean to you?

How does Christ's power to set free the prisoners of death give you hope?

DAY 07

ANGELS & ARCHANGELS

I arise today
through the strength
of the love of cherubim,
in the obedience of angels,
in the service of archangels

Cherubim… Angels… Archangels…

Do not neglect to show hospitality to strangers, for by doing that some have entertained angels without knowing it (Hebrews 13:2).

Angels represent one of those aspects of faith that range from mysterious to misunderstood to entirely veiled in fantasy. The cute little baby cherubs from Hallmark are a far cry from the winged cherubim of Genesis 3 who guard the garden of Eden with flaming swords. We might hear a bell in "It's a Wonderful Life" when an angel gets wings, but not so much in real life.[6] And while many people might tell us that heaven needs another angel when our loved one passes away, there is no biblical evidence that humans become angels. Rather, we are glorified and restored to the perfect image of God in which we were first created. The same cannot be said for angels.

While we may not fully understand them, angels are entirely different spiritual beings. They often appear in human form such as the messengers who announced to Abraham and Sarah that they would have a child (Genesis 18). They appear in visions around the throne room of the Most High, though they themselves are not to be worshipped (Isaiah 6, Revelation 22:8-9). Archangels like Gabriel and Michael are explicitly named in extraordinary circumstances (Luke 1:19, Daniel 10:21, 12:1).

With all the mystery surrounding angels, one thing is clear: God uses them as messengers and servants to communicate with humanity. Often their appearance is made known when God requires an extraordinary response of obedience such as Mary's willingness to

---

[6] Frank Capra, *It's a Wonderful Life* (Paramount, 1946).

become the mother of the Son of God. This isn't the kind of message one might entrust to just any ordinary courier or a post on social media.

Regardless of the form they take, two things are certain about angels. First, as servants of God, they act as an extension of God's love for us. The cherubim who guarded the garden, for example, prevented Adam and Eve from eating from the tree of life and thereby living forever in the brokenness and misery of sin. God had a bigger plan for restoration that required both death and resurrection. Secondly, because angels serve the Lord as an extension of God's love, their word is always trustworthy and true.

I cannot honestly say that I've explicitly heard a word from an angel, although there have been seemingly random people who have crossed my path for a short time with a profound word from God for a particular season or situation in life. Perhaps in this sense we have all encountered angels. We have all received messages from God. This is an angel's primary task. Angels deliver messages from heaven.

This seemingly obscure part of St. Patrick's prayer may be crucial in our journey to become echoes of the whispers of heaven. We must first arise in the love of cherubim, in the obedience of angels and in the service of archangels, that we might hear and discern these messages from heaven and obey them fully on earth.

As we seek to become more aware of the work of angels in our midst, let us simply pray as Mary prayed in response to the angelic host…

> "Here am I, the servant of the Lord; let it be with me according to your word" (Luke 1:38).

Reflections:

What experience, if any, have you had with angels in your life?

How do you feel about the idea that you may be "entertaining angels unaware?"

In what ways do the presence of angels impact your faith and give you strength?

DAY 08

RESURRECTION & REWARD

I arise today
in the hope of resurrection
to meet with reward

The word of the Lord came to Abram in a vision: "Do not be afraid, Abram. I am your shield, your very great reward" (Genesis 15:1, NIV).

Similarly, Jesus declares to Mary,

Jesus said to her, "I am the resurrection and the life. Those who believe in me, even though they die, will live… (John 11:25).

Notice that Jesus doesn't tell Mary he will raise up Lazarus. In fact, he doesn't directly promise to bring anyone back from the dead. He simply declares that he *is* the resurrection. Likewise, God does not promise Abram a material reward for his faithfulness. The very presence of God is all the reward Abram could ask for and more.

Where do we place our hope? We often talk about heaven as a place free from pain where we will reunite with our loved ones. We think of our eternal reward in terms of fixing what was broken on earth and healing all our hurt and sorrow. God certainly provides these things, but what if our hope for eternity is too small?

I once heard it said that we spend so much time grabbing for the gifts held out in God's hands that we never stop to look upon God's face. I think that is why God says to Abram, "I am your reward," and why Jesus says that he is the resurrection. All these blessings, even the gift of eternal life itself, have no substance apart from the presence of God.

> For from him and through him and to him are all things. To him be glory forever. Amen (Romans 11:36).

What if we died and experienced the gift of resurrection, but never saw Jesus on the other side? What if everything we know about heaven is true, except that God wasn't actually there? What if it was just some grand endless party where we get to hang out with those we loved on earth and everyone else who has gone before, but there was no divine presence?

I know the idea of heaven without Jesus is about as heretical as it gets, and this is certainly not my intent. But hypothetically, if it were possible to go to heaven and find that Jesus decided not to live there, how long would it take for us to notice? How long would we be content enjoying all our rewards before we began to feel like something was missing.

Now let's bring that idea a little closer to home. When we go to church and hang out with our friends and family, do we intentionally look around to see where Jesus is present? Are there some weeks we walk out of worship never having noticed the one we came to glorify? What about our daily lives? Is Jesus the first reward we hope for every morning when we wake up, or are there other more pressing things we must strive to gain that day?

In all the blessings we pray for and all the rewards we hope for, let us not hope and pray too small. Let us not settle for anything less than arising and living each day fully in the presence of the one who is both our resurrection and our great reward.

Reflections:

What kinds of rewards do you hope for in heaven? How might your hopes be too small?

Have you ever gone to church without consciously seeking an encounter with Christ? What was that experience like?

In what ways do you find yourself reaching for what's in God's hands instead of gazing upon God's face?

DAY 09

SAINTS

I arise today
in the prayers of patriarchs,
in the predictions of prophets,
in the preaching of apostles,
in the faith of confessors,
in the innocence of holy virgins,
in the deeds of righteous men

As we wrap up this segment of the Breastplate prayer, we arise in the strength of the Great Cloud of Witnesses described in Hebrews 12.

In the Catholic tradition of St. Patrick, these witnesses are broken into several groups, some more familiar than others.

I arise today in the prayers of patriarchs…

Here we look back to the earliest saints like Abraham, Isaac and Jacob. They acted in faith and obedience before there was a church or temple system to follow, before the law was written, and even before the world had any concept that there may only be one God. They were not perfect, but they were the trailblazers of faith who truly knew what it meant to walk with God. Their prayers echo through the ages and invite us deeper into the heart of a God who desires to be known.

How might we live out their example of faith?

I arise today in the predictions of prophets…

The prophets spoke the words of the Lord and yet were often ignored and persecuted. They called the people to repentance and to the work of mercy and justice for all. They foretold a highway in the wilderness that God would build to bring us home long before we ever realized we were lost (Isaiah 40:3).

How might we respond to their voices challenging us today?

I arise in the preaching of apostles…

As we move into the New Testament, we find apostles or "sent ones," who walked with Jesus and scattered throughout the world to baptize, teach, and make disciples, proclaiming the Good News of God's Kingdom on earth (Matthew 28:19-20).

How are we continuing in the apostolic witness, proclaiming the good news of Christ and making disciples for the transformation of our world?

I arise in the faith of confessors and in the innocence of holy virgins…

Confessors and holy virgins are far less familiar to protestant ears. They generally refer to the Saints of God. With deep faith, confessors vow their absolute allegiance to Christ even through great hardship and persecution. Holy virgins refer specifically to the women who took vows of innocence or chastity that they might be the spouse of Christ alone. In both cases, these are saints who maintain an exceptional degree of holiness and purity. They set themselves apart from the world for the sake of their exclusive service to the Lord.

In what ways do our own faith and purity reflect that of these great saints who have gone before? How are we living pure and holy lives?

I arise in the deeds of righteous men.

The "deeds of righteous men" encapsulates all we have seen in the holy and righteous examples of the saints. Granted, the gender exclusivity is a product of St. Patrick's time, but the implication is the same. God calls every man, woman and child to a life of righteousness and declares that God's children will be known by their acts of love. "Faith without works (or deeds) is dead" (James 2:17).

Will others recognize that we are children of God by our righteous deeds and acts of selfless love?

Reflections:

Consider the questions raised after each category of saints. What are some of the ways God is strengthening you through the Saints even now?

How might the Spirit be using their examples to convict, to challenge, and to call you more fully into a holy life?

How might arising each day in the faith of that great cloud of witnesses help you as you run the race Paul describes in 2 Timothy 4:7?

DAY 10

HEAVEN

*I arise today
through the strength of heaven*

As the old country song says, "Everybody wants to go to heaven, but nobody wants to die."[7] I've heard preachers say that they are overjoyed about the idea of going to heaven, but they don't want to be on the next busload.

The apostle Paul writes:

> For to me, living is Christ and dying is gain. If I am to

---

[7] Kenny Chesney, "Everybody Wants to Go to Heaven" (BNA Records, 2008). Written by Marty Dotson & Jim Collins.

live in the flesh, that means fruitful labor for me; and I do not know which I prefer. I am hard pressed between the two: my desire is to depart and be with Christ, for that is far better; but to remain in the flesh is more necessary for you (Philippians 1:21-24).

If heaven is such a joyful prospect and we all desire to be there, why do we want to delay our arrival? They say Disney World is the "most magical place on earth," but if I tell my 5-year-old daughter we are going there one day, she does not respond with, "That sounds great Daddy, but no rush. Maybe one day we can go after I'm old and tired and worn out." Of course not. She wants to go NOW, if not sooner.

She asked me about heaven the other day because having two parents in pastoral ministry exposes her to the realities of sickness and death on a regular basis. I told her it was even better than Disney and she asked two very important questions. First, "Will there be rides?" and second, "Will Anna and Elsa be there?" (from Disney's *Frozen*). At least she has her priorities straight. On the other hand, she has also said on many occasions that she can't wait to go to heaven so she can see Jesus.

That's the beauty of today's prayer. We don't have to wait until we get to heaven to see Jesus. The strength of heaven is not found in death, but in life.

Thy kingdom come, thy will be done, on earth as it is in heaven (Matthew 6:10, KJV).

It is easy to sit around watching Christian movies on TV as if the earth is nothing more than one giant waiting room until it's our turn to enter the pearly gates. If we fall into this trap of Christian comfort, who will work to fulfill Jesus command to proclaim God's Kingdom on earth as it is in heaven?

"I arise TODAY in the strength of heaven."

Jesus proclaimed that the Kingdom of Heaven is at hand (Mark 1:15).

As Michael Gungor sings, "I don't know what you've been told, but heaven is coming down to the world."[8]

> Then I saw a new heaven and a new earth; for the first heaven and the first earth had passed away, and the sea was no more. And I saw the holy city, the new Jerusalem, coming down out of heaven from God, prepared as a bride adorned for her husband.
>
> And I heard a loud voice from the throne saying,
>
> > "See, the home of God is among mortals.
> > He will dwell with them;

---

[8] Michael Gungor, "Heaven" (Brash Music, 2010).

> they will be his peoples,
> and God himself will be with them;
> he will wipe every tear from their eyes.
> Death will be no more;
> mourning and crying and pain will be no more,
> for the first things have passed away"
> (Revelation 21:1-4).

What are we waiting for?

Let the Kingdom of Heaven come upon the earth as it is in heaven.

Let us rejoice that God has chosen to dwell among us through the presence of the Holy Spirit.

Let us not wait until we are in the grave to arise in the strength of heaven, but let us arise TODAY and walk with Jesus Christ, Lord of heaven and earth.

Let us open our eyes to the glorious presence of God's Kingdom, that we may proclaim this good news to the world and that all might work together to bring about the fullness of the reign of Christ on earth as it is in heaven.

Reflections:

Do you think of heaven primarily as a future dwelling place or a present reality?

How do you experience the tension between wanting to "go to heaven" and "not wanting to die"?

In what ways is God calling you to live in the strength of heaven today?

DAY 11

SUN

> I arise today
> through the light of the sun

St Patrick died on the 17th of March, 493. In his Confession he writes:

> For the sun we see rises each day for us at His command, but it will never reign, neither will its splendor last, but all who worship it will come wretchedly to punishment. We, on the other hand, shall not die, who believe in and worship the true sun, Christ, who will never die, no more shall he die who has done Christ's will, but will abide forever just as

Christ abides forever, who reigns with God the Father Almighty and with the Holy Spirit before the beginning of time and now and forever and ever. Amen.[9]

Throughout history the image of the sun has represented "God" and in many cultures and religions, the sun itself is worshiped as the highest god. To ancient people who did not have satellites and cameras in space to explain the heavenly bodies, it is no wonder the sun would command such power and awe. Think about it. For life on earth, the sun controls everything.

The sun gives us light by which to see, work and live. Yet it is so bright that no one can look directly upon it. The rhythms of day and night provide our bodies with appropriate rest and awaken us to enjoy the life we are given.

The sun provides warmth to keep animals, crops, and people from freezing to death in colder climates.

Fruits and vegetables grow heartier when there is plenty of sunlight. While rain is also necessary, too much can flood the fields and wash out the harvest. The sun is needed to dry things out before it rains again. This cycle of sun and rain is crucial to our survival. Too much or too little of either is detrimental.

---

[9] Holmes, *The Real Saint Patrick*. 83.

In modern times we have learned a great deal about the necessity and the power of the sun. Through the technology of solar panels, we have harnessed the power of the sun as a source of tremendous renewable energy. The sun has enough energy to power our entire planet with no drain on our natural resources. There is nothing we as humans can do to burn out the energy of the sun. In so many ways, the sun serves as both the source and the sustainer of life. No wonder the god of the sun stood above so many other gods in ancient times.

For the people of ancient Ireland, it was no different. Patrick did not try to argue against them. In fact, the circle we see at the center of the Celtic Cross acknowledges the significance of the sun. Yet, when juxtaposed with the cross, it takes on new meaning.

While the sun is indeed great, it is not great in and of itself. Rather, the sun is a gift from a greater source. The Son of God died upon the cross so that we might come before the throne of the very one who spoke the sun into existence.

Therefore, let us arise with joy in the light of the sun. Let the sun's warmth bring a smile upon our face and the sun's light guide us through the day. Let the setting of the sun grant us peace and rest through the night and comfort in the knowledge that it will rise again.

But in all of this, let us worship and bow down to the Creator of the sun, who gave us this tremendous gift. "Let there be light," God said… and before anything else came into being, there was light. And God said it was good.

Let us arise today in the light of the sun and walk by the light of the Son of the Most High.

Reflections:

Meditate on a time when you found yourself in awe at the beauty and glory of the sun, perhaps a particular sunrise or sunset. What meaning did that time have for you?

How does the sun direct your attention to the Creator and remind you of the Son of God?

People will turn their lives upside down just to catch a glimpse of the sun during a solar eclipse. What would it look like if we were as intentional about seeking the face of Christ, the Son of God, in every person we meet?

DAY 12

MOON

*I arise today
through the radiance of moon*

Interesting that the writer of this prayer mentions only the simple "light" of the sun, and yet describes the moon as "radiant."

Radiance implies more than mere light. It envisions brightness, splendor, brilliance. If anything, this seems more appropriate for the sun than the moon. After all, the moon shines with a much softer, gentler glow. We cannot even look upon the brilliance of the sun but the moon we can watch clearly from its rising to its setting with no ill effect.

Perhaps the difference is context. It's easy to take the sun for granted because when it shines, all is light, and we never look directly at the source. The moon shines more like a candle in the darkness. Rather than illuminating all we see around us; its glow draws our eyes across the darkness of the night sky to the source of the light. Against the dark of night, the moon is indeed radiant, especially when it is full or in some special state like a super-moon or harvest moon.

The moon does not produce its own light but reflects the light of the sun upon us on the earth.

While the sun is a glorious metaphor for the brilliantly blinding light of Holy God, the moon perhaps offers a metaphor for our place as God's children in the darkness of a sinful world. When God's light shines upon us, every crack and crevice is exposed just as the sun illuminates every crater and ridge on the moon's landscape. Though we try to hide in the darkness, the world needs to see that even in our brokenness we are still beautiful to the Creator. Every crater, or scar, tells a story. Every crack we see on the face of another reminds us that we are not alone. God has sustained us through every meteor impact we have faced.

As we turn our face to the light, we must reflect that light into the darkness of the world. When we try to shine like the sun, exposing the cracks on the surface of others, people turn away in fear, shame, or even anger. But when we reflect the light and allow others to draw near, we can bask in the glow of the Son of God and together radiate even more light into the darkness.

One final thought. The moon has little value during the day. We do not see its light. Therefore, if we are to reflect the radiance of the moon in a way that will bring light and hope to others, we must enter their darkness. We cannot hide in well-lit sanctuaries where our scars are so easily washed out by the glare. In the moonlight we find a safe place to be real without being blinded. In the moonlight we discover that despite our scars, we are beautiful and even radiant as we reflect the glory of the Son, in whom all things are created and have their being.

Reflections:

Spend some time gazing at the moon. What do you feel? How do you see yourself? How do you see God?

How does your life reflect the glory and the love of God?

In what ways have we turned our face away from the blinding light of the Son and no longer reflect His radiance? How might you reflect God's light today?

DAY 13

FIRE

I arise today
through the splendor of fire

Like the sun and moon, the splendor of fire calls forth images of brightness, radiance and glorious light. Yet just as the softness of the moon's reflective glow adds another dimension to the glorious light of God, the warm crackle of a dancing fire takes us even deeper into the meaning of God's light

Imagine yourself sitting before a stone fireplace or a blazing campfire. Do you have any fond memories gathered around a fire with loved ones? Such memories can take us back to serene moments in our lives when we found ourselves lost in the fire's dance.

Fire is practical and necessary for life; to cook, keep warm, cleanse or purify and so on. We use fire in so many ways, but these functions do not define the fire itself.

Fire is mysterious, beautiful, and inviting, though it can become equally dangerous and destructive. There is no exact science in determining where or in which direction each flare will rise from its source. Likewise, we cannot anticipate when Holy Spirit's fiery tongue may fall upon us and ignite us in ways that our safe and solitary upper rooms can no longer contain.

The splendor of fire has a way of both drawing us together and calling us to silence. We begin an evening around a campfire with laughter and storytelling as we roast hot dogs and marshmallows, but in the end, even the most talkative people find themselves gazing quietly into the mystery of the slowly dying embers. Perhaps the life of the fire calls us to reflect upon the splendor of our own lives, once so active and full of energy but eventually we all slow down to rest.

While attending a silent retreat, I noticed how the stone hearth in the retreat center invited every participant to sit in its warm glow even as frost overtook the ground just outside the window. Some would read, others slept. Some poked at the logs to stir up the embers while other sat and stared. Though its strength grew and faded in cycles throughout the day, it kept burning until the doors were locked for the night. It did not speak audibly like the burning bush on God's Holy Mountain, yet its voice whispered divine mysteries in the language of the heart and soul.

It is fitting that James describes the tongue as a fire and that the Holy Spirit comes in tongues of fire, for fire indeed has a voice (James 3:5-6, Acts 2:1-13). Like the flames themselves, the voice can speak warmth and comfort, or it can consume all that is in its path like a raging forest fire. The fire itself is not alive, nor is God contained in the fire any more than God is in the rocks or trees or even in the sun or the moon. But there was a reason all these elements of earth and sky were sacred to the Celtic people and there is a reason St. Patrick and others did not entirely exclude these phenomena from Christian worship. If God is indeed the creator of all things, why would we not expect to see glimpses of the divine nature, character and purposes in that which God created?

We don't listen to the fire or dance with the flames, but we are invited to hear and to dance with the God of the flames and perhaps, like Shadrach Meshach and Abednego, even to stand with the Son of God in the midst of the fire and not be consumed (Daniel 3).

Reflections:

Spend some time gazing at a fire. What do you feel? How do you see yourself? How do you see God?

What do you hear God speaking to you through the fire and how might the Three-One God be inviting you to participate in the dance?

In your life right now, would you describe the Holy Spirit's presence more like a blaze, a fading ember, or somewhere in between? Why?

DAY 14

LIGHTNING

I arise today
through the speed of lightning

So many attributes of lightning remained unknown to St. Patrick and his contemporaries. The electromagnetic properties within this strange phenomenon were inconceivable to the Celtic people and indeed to all the ancient world. Yet one simple observation is clear… lightning strikes fast.

We now know that a flash of lightning averages around

93,000 miles per second.[10] Pre-modern people, however, did not need to understand the speed of light or the nature of electricity to recognize this as one of, if not the fastest observable phenomenon in nature.

What is the significance of such speed in relation to our life with God? God may be present everywhere at once, but we do not wake up one day empowered by the Holy Spirit to run like the Flash, nor is God running around from place to place like a squirrel on Red Bull trying to keep up with all the cries for help sent up into the sky like prayerful bat-signals.

In fact, God's omnipresent nature makes speed entirely irrelevant. Speed is a measurement of motion, but God is often described as the "unmoved mover".[11] In other words, God may set creation in motion and move people to action in response to divine promptings, but God is not moved. God simply is. If there is no place that God is not, there is nowhere for God to move, at least not in a physical sense.

Speed also requires a relationship between motion and time. How fast something moves is determined by how much time passes as the object moves from one place to another. Just like space, time is also an irrelevant concept

---

[10] "Lightning Facts and Statistics," *WeatherImagery* (blog), February 18, 2007, http://www.weatherimagery.com/blog/lightning-facts/.
[11] "Aristotle - The Unmoved Mover," Encyclopedia Britannica, accessed October 17, 2019, https://www.britannica.com/biography/Aristotle.

for God. In theological terms, we might say that God exists in the "Eternal Now".[12] From the creation of the world to the final consummation in the New Jerusalem... even this very moment in which you find yourself reading an obscure reflection on speed and time... each and every moment exists as a "present moment" for God. Time does not pass in eternity. Just as speed requires a starting place and an ending place, so the measurement of time requires a beginning and an end. God has neither. There was never a time when God was not and there will never be a time when God ceases to exist.

Are you utterly confused yet? Is your brain spinning with this impossible concept?

If so, you are in good company. Our inability to conceive of a reality not limited by space and time reminds us of our mortality and the futility of trying to fully comprehend or explain the nature of God or eternity. We simply do not have the language to speak of such things. God is God. We are not.

If speed has no meaning outside of space and time and therefore has no meaning for God who exists outside of space and time, what does it mean to arise today with the speed of lightning?

---

[12] Paul Tillich, *The Eternal Now* (New York: Charles Scribner's Sons, 1963).

Here is my limited and perhaps foolish attempt at an explanation, or at least what the image seems to imply to me.

A flash of lightning, to a non-scientific eye, is an observable phenomenon that defies time and space. It flashes so fast that perhaps it is the closest we can come to understanding how fast a "day" might be from God's eternal point of view. For whether we are talking about a day or a thousand years, both pass as quickly as a bolt of lightning through the lens of eternity.

What if to arise through the speed of lightning is simply to arise with an eternal perspective? All the worries of yesterday, today and tomorrow do not consume us because compared to eternity, even the worst of our problems is a fleeting reality, gone as fast as it came.

To be in Christ is to live in the light of eternity, and in this light, we find hope. Even when time seems to stop and our suffering feels like it will never end, we can arise through the speed of lightning and celebrate Christ's final victory in the hope and joy of an eternity that has already begun.

Reflections:

Reflect on a time when you just sat and watched a lightning storm. Describe your thoughts and feelings as you watched the lightning flash.

How do you understand the "speed of lightning" in your own relationship with God?

Meditate on 2 Peter 3:8-9. Write down what is God speaking to your heart?

DAY 15

WIND

*I arise today
through the swiftness of wind*

Like lightning, wind offers another image for speed, and with it, another nuance to explore in our understanding of Creator God.

Swiftness implies something more graceful than lightning, like a speed skater on the ice or a deer swiftly darting through the forest glade. While the speed of lightning is sharp, focused, direct and intense, wind flows in graceful rhythms. Even strong sustained winds like that of a hurricane more closely resemble the ebb and flow of ocean waves than a lightning strike or a Formula 1 racecar.

Wind and lightning have radically different effects. Take the sail of a ship for example. Wind fills the sail and guides the ship, if we point the sail in the right direction. A lightning strike on that same sail would set the ship ablaze.

Wind is fluid. Wind blows where it wills. We can harness the energy of the wind, but we cannot create it, control it, or contain it. We see the image of wind along with tongues of fire at Pentecost as the Holy Spirit blows through the upper room and fills the disciples with divine strength, boldness, and understanding (Acts 2:1-13).

Wind involves the rapid movement of air from an area of high pressure to an area of low pressure, much like the compressed air inside a balloon being released into wide open atmosphere. This image is rich with spiritual implications. How can we expect the "wind" or "breath" of God's Spirit to flow into us if we live in a constant state of "high pressure", always forcing air out rather than being empty enough to receive it?

The beautifully poetic word for wind in Hebrew, "Ruach," also means spirit and breath. As we arise through the swiftness of wind, the Spirit of the Lord breathes life into our physical bodies and animates our spirits. "In Him we live and move and have our being" (Acts 17:28). While Luke refers explicitly to Christ, we experience the life of Christ through the movement of the Holy Spirit, much like we experience the existence of invisible pressure systems through the movement of the wind.

Sermons upon sermons could be and have been written about the metaphor of wind as it relates to God and our spiritual lives. I offer only a glimpse of the many ways we might meditate upon this image. May the wind of God's Spirit fill the sails of our Holy Imagination and lead us where God wills, to whatever dead and dying places need to be awakened by divine CPR.

One final thought. Wind often serves as an indicator of greater realities. The strength and direction of the wind helps us determine the location, speed, and direction of approaching storms. When the wind is too intense, we must "hunker down" and weather the storm. When the wind is too still, we might call it "the calm before the storm" or perhaps even find ourselves "in the eye of the storm". When the wind blows as a warm and gentle spring breeze, we feel relaxed and at peace.

If wind and breath and spirit are so intimately related, perhaps our own breath can serve as a barometer of our spiritual condition. We don't pay much attention to our breathing unless we have overexerted ourselves or find ourselves struggling to breathe.

Take time to notice the Spirit-wind of your own breath.

> Is it swift and graceful, like that skater gliding with ease across the ice, or does it feel sharp, heavy, shallow, or difficult?

Take a deep breath.

> What do you feel?
>
> Does this sensation seem unfamiliar or natural?
>
> How does it feel as you exhale?
>
> What feelings are you exhaling with this deep breath?

Reflections:

How do you experience the swiftness of wind in your own life right now?

Which image or description of wind most resonates with your Holy Imagination right now? What might God be speaking to you through this image?

How would you describe your own breathing in this moment? What is the Holy Spirit whispering to you through your own breath?

DAY 16

SEA

*I arise today
through the depth of the sea*

Deep calls to deep in the roar of your waterfalls; all your waves and breakers have swept over me (Psalm 42:7, NIV).

The Message paraphrase of this Psalm translates "deep" to "chaos."

Chaos calls to chaos, to the tune of whitewater rapids… (Psalm 42:7a, MSG).

Throughout the book of Revelation, the sea represents the realm of darkness, evil, and chaos. Ancient people viewed the sea as the place of unknown, a place filled with frightening mysteries. Whether by "sea monsters" or simply "falling off the edge of the earth," many sailors never returned from this untamed place. St. Patrick understood this fearful image of the sea all too well. As a teenager, Irish raiders from across the sea captured him and forced him into slavery.[13]

Yet in this poetic cry to God, we don't find the sea portrayed as a dark place. Rather we are called to arise not only through the sea, but through "the depth of sea."

We exert so much energy in life trying to avoid the "deep," steering clear of chaos as much as possible. We often swerve past one chaotic situation only to find ourselves in an even darker and more difficult place. We cannot control the chaos. We cannot avoid the "deep." It simply exists.

Arising through the depths helps us acknowledge this reality and respond with hope instead of despair, with courage instead of fear, with peace instead of stress. As the Psalmist writes, "If I make my bed in the depths, you are there" (Psalm 139:8, NIV). Even when we find ourselves wallowing in the depths of our pain or sorrow, God can still be found in the chaos.

---

[13] Holmes, *The Real Saint Patrick*.

There is little use in elaborating on "the depths" of the seas we experience. We know these dark and chaotic places all too well. Today our prayer invites us to embrace those depths and to find God amid the chaos.

Let us meditate on Psalm 42, a cry to God from the deepest and darkest places within.

Psalm 42 (NIV)

> As the deer pants for streams of water,
>   so my soul pants for you, my God.
> My soul thirsts for God, for the living God.
>   When can I go and meet with God?
> My tears have been my food
>   day and night,
> while people say to me all day long,
>   "Where is your God?"
> These things I remember
>   as I pour out my soul:
> how I used to go to the house of God
>   under the protection of the Mighty One
> with shouts of joy and praise
>   among the festive throng.
>
> Why, my soul, are you downcast?
>   Why so disturbed within me?
> Put your hope in God,
>   for I will yet praise him,
>   my Savior and my God.

My soul is downcast within me;
    therefore I will remember you
from the land of the Jordan,
    the heights of Hermon—from Mount Mizar.
Deep calls to deep
    in the roar of your waterfalls;
all your waves and breakers
    have swept over me.
By day the Lord directs his love,
    at night his song is with me—
    a prayer to the God of my life.
I say to God my Rock,
    "Why have you forgotten me?
Why must I go about mourning,
    oppressed by the enemy?"
My bones suffer mortal agony
    as my foes taunt me,
saying to me all day long,
    "Where is your God?"
Why, my soul, are you downcast?
    Why so disturbed within me?
Put your hope in God,
    for I will yet praise him,
    my Savior and my God.

Reflections:

Ask God to examine your heart and reveal the deepest places of chaos. If a circumstance comes to mind, ask God to help you go deeper. Where is the underlying chaos in the depths of your heart and soul?

In what ways do you find yourself trying to avoid the depths? Reflect on a time when you embraced the depth and where you saw God present in that place.

Meditate on Psalm 42. Also consider Psalm 139. What is the Holy Spirit speaking to your soul?

DAY 17

EARTH

I arise today
through the stability of earth

One of the most beautiful and refreshing things about this series on St. Patrick's Breastplate Prayer is the ability to simply listen to the Spirit and reflect on whatever God brings to my heart and mind without trying to dissect every thought through a grueling process of research and study. Study is important and I enjoy academic rigor, but there is something to be said for responding to "first thoughts" on a word, a phrase, a scripture passage, an image, an experience, or anything else through which God chooses to speak.

I see it as the spiritual or written equivalent of the #nofilter hashtag often used in photography. Rather than an academic essay on Patrick's Prayer, these reflections are more like journal entries, offering those "first thoughts" and reflections and allowing God to use them as the Spirit wills (#nofilter).

This approach is not without risk, but there is also is also great joy and freedom in following the stream of consciousness wherever it leads, like dancing with the Spirit and allowing God to lead, rather than relying on my own reason and understanding.

Today, this approach ran me into a bit of a problem. I wrote an entire reflection on the stability of earth using the image of the solid rock on which we stand secure. As I began writing for the next day, I typed the next line of the prayer… "I arise today through the firmness of rock."

Oops. I got ahead of myself. Tomorrow's reflection on the firmness of rock is actually the reflection I wrote for today.

This of course leaves me in a bit of a bind. What do I write for today about arising through the "stability of earth"?

Honestly, I'm not sure. When I think of the stability of earth, my mind immediately jumps to the image of rocks.

Yet in this prayer, rock and earth remain two distinct images despite their many similarities.

When I think of earth as distinct from rock, stability is not the word that comes to mind. Other than various types of rock, earth consists of softer substances like soil, sand, clay, grass and peat. Earth tends to give a little under our feet. When it is wet it may wash out completely, like the sinking sand that quite literally washes out from under your feet as you stand on the beach. Have you ever tried to mow the grass after a good rain? As the tires spin in the mud, stability is the last word I would use to describe "earth."

So now I wonder, is there another way to look at "earth?"

Earth is not only the ground; it is the entire planet which humanity inhabits. It is the Garden of Eden and it is Fallen Babylon. It is natural and it is man-made. It is forests and deserts and arctic tundra, and it is villages, parks and cities. The earth is ecosystems and climate change and the food chain and the "circle of life." Earth may very well represent all life as we know it.

What if, just for a moment, we consider earth as less about the ground itself and more about the place where life thrives? Earth is a habitat designed for everything God would create. Perhaps in this sense, earth is more stable than we think. Yes, parts of the earth are destroyed by fire, floods, earthquakes and even unnatural human forces. Yes, species have gone extinct and the cycle of life and death never ends. Earth and all that is on it exists in a constant state of flux.

Yet the earth still spins on its axis. It maintains its orbit around the sun century after century and millennium after millennium, at least close enough to sustain life but not too close to destroy it.

What if stability does not depend on keeping everything the same? What if stability is not the absence of change or the firmness of our foundations, but rather our ability to withstand an ever-changing reality and even grow and thrive from it? Just like a tall building must have a bit of give to withstand high winds or earthquakes, so the earth with all its shifting sands, remains a stable sanctuary in which we can live and breathe and sing the praises of our Creator.

Reflections:

What does stability mean to you considering all the shifts and changes in life?

How do you understand the "stability of earth" and how does your understanding resonate with your life right now?

Pick out a line from this prayer, or perhaps a word or phrase from a scripture you recently read and allow your stream-of-consciousness to flow freely with it. What "first thoughts" is the Spirit laying on your heart? How is God calling you to respond? #nofilter

DAY 18

ROCK

> I arise today
> Through the firmness of rock

We often describe the Christian life as diving into deeper waters, allowing ourselves to be caught up in the wind and waves of the Spirit. This is an important truth, but not the whole truth. Yes, life in the Spirit can often seem like a mighty rushing river, but God is also our rock and our salvation, a mighty fortress and a bulwark never failing.[14]

---

[14] Martin Luther, "A Mighty Fortress Is Our God", 1529.

I've been to many mountain overlooks throughout North Carolina and Kentucky and most of the popular touristy ones are blocked off with man-made rails to keep people from falling over the edge. My favorite places in the mountains are on the rocks beyond the rails. There is one area like this at Grandfather Mountain, NC, on the far side of a suspension bridge. I've also hiked a few rock arches without rails in Red River Gorge, Kentucky. My favorite by far is the top of Table Mountain in Cape Town, South Africa. For pictures, check out the digital resource page on my website found below.[15]

It's the largest mountaintop I have ever hiked, and the views over the ocean are awe-inspiring. That's what I like most about it. Unlike the Smoky Mountains on my home turf, this mountain seems to rise right out of the sea. I sat on the edge of a rock overlooking the sea for well over an hour. As I looked down at the inner city of Cape Town and to the harbor and sea beyond, I thought about the turmoil the nation had gone through, the suffering and injustice they experienced under Apartheid, the continual rises and falls of governments, the people on the margins who endure the brunt of the decisions made by those on top who are rarely affected. This kind of chaos exists in every nation, but the rock I sat upon reminded me that no matter how hard the waves crashed against the base of the mountain, the ground above it all remained solid.

---

[15] "I Arise Today – Resources," Echo, https://www.craigsefa.org/arise/resources. Day 18.

I also remember standing on the Cliffs of Mohr along Ireland's Atlantic coast. I heard the rough surf below but could not see anything through the dense fog. We couldn't even see the cliff walls below us. Yet somehow these invisible rocks jutting out of the sea stood firm against centuries of crashing waves and winds.

When the winds of life throw me off balance and the waves crash hard against the foundations I thought were secure, these are the places I long to be. I remember standing on the edge of Chimney Rock in Kentucky one April afternoon. A random late year snowstorm blew in out of nowhere, but as the wind pressed against me and the snow blinded my view, I became even more aware of the solid rock beneath my feet.

"Why do we run from the rain," I wrote in a song that day. "Why do we hide from the storm?"[16]

The rock is secure. There is nothing to fear. The ground is firm beneath our feet.

My prayer for the church and for all of us is that we will not only stand firm on the solid rock of Christ, but that we will become a place of stability where others can sit or stand secure even in the midst of their storms, far above the crashing waves of life.

---

[16] Craig Sefa, "Feel My Pain", 2007.

It is one thing to take shelter inside where we cannot see or hear the waves and wind or feel the rain and snow. Sometimes, however, we need to spend some time in the middle of the churning sea or feel the wind and rain upon our skin as we sit or stand on the solid rock. The shelters we build to hide ourselves from the world will inevitably crumble, but the mountain stands secure.

Reflections:

Where do you need a firm rock in your life right now?

In response to storms, do you tend to retreat to a self-made shelter or stand strong on the mountain to face it? How do you sense God leading you to respond to the storms in your life today?

Would people describe you as a rock in their life, a safe and firm place where they can feel secure no matter what they are dealing with? Who might God be calling you to be a rock for this week? Who has God put in your life to be a rock for you?

DAY 19

PILOT

*I arise today
through God's strength to pilot me...*

In the movie "Cool Runnings," Sanka is the best pushcart derby driver in Jamaica. When his friend Derice starts a Jamaican bobsled team, Sanka assumes he will drive the bobsled. Here is the coach's response:

> Irv: You see Sanka, the driver has to work harder than anyone. He's the first to show up, and the last to leave. When his buddies are all out drinking beer, he's up in his room studying pictures of turns. You see, a driver must remain focused one hundred percent at all times.

Not only is he responsible for knowing every inch of every course he races, he's also responsible for the lives of the other men in the sled. Now do you want that responsibility?

Sanka Coffie: I say we make Derice the driver.

Irv: So do I, Sanka. So do I.[17]

A pilot steers the ship. He or she essentially functions as "the driver". In an age where nearly everyone drives a car and even aircraft fly on "automatic pilot", we can easily take the pilot's role for granted. After all, steering isn't that hard. We do it every day. And just like a plane, sometimes we end up running on autopilot. Have you ever had that moment when you pull into the driveway at home and realize you don't even remember making the last several turns? It's easy to zone out somewhere along the all too familiar route.

We have the same problem when we try to steer, drive, or pilot our lives. We make a thousand choices a day in our familiar routines without a second thought. We react to input and circumstances almost involuntarily rather than pausing to intentionally consider our response.

The strength of a pilot is a mental strength, the strength of a disciplined and focused mind. Such single-minded

---

[17] Jon Turteltaub, *Cool Runnings* (Walt Disney Pictures, 1993). Dialog between — Irv Blitzer (John Candy) and Sanka Coffie (Doug E. Doug)

focus does not come naturally in a world that turns our attention from one thing to the next at a pace that would give anyone whiplash. As Sanka learned in the movie, it is one thing to steer a pushcart down a dirt hill, but it is entirely something else to steer a metal sled barreling through gut wrenching turns down an icy track.

Life is more like a bobsled track than a wide-open downhill slope. We must constantly stay alert. The slightest missed turn can cause unintentional harm to ourselves and those riding with us in the sled. The ability to make such split-second decisions does not come in the moment. It comes from all those hours of training and study. Over time, we learn to respond with grace and truth as naturally as we navigate the familiar roads to our homes.

I know a bobsled driver is not exactly what the writer had in mind when he talks of a pilot, but there is one more parallel worth exploring. Unlike flying with an airline pilot, the "passengers" in a bobsled are not passive. They do not sit back sipping on sodas and eating pretzels while the driver or "pilot" does all the work. They must stay low and lean in with the pilot through every curve. Each person in the sled must be in sync with the drivers every move.

Likewise, the people on ancient sailing ships could not sit back and wait until the captain, or "pilot", steered them safely into port. There was much work to be done: sails to be hoisted, ropes to be tied, and decks to be cleaned, along with a hundred other responsibilities which I know nothing about. The pilot may have the strength and focus to keep the ship on course, but the pilot doesn't work alone. We must train and discipline ourselves with the strength and focus to follow the pilot's lead.

To paraphrase Sanka, "I say we make God the driver."

Reflections:

In what ways do you try to pilot your own life? How do you feel about the results? How is it working for you?

What fears prevent you from giving God complete control of the wheel?

What habits or disciplines might God be calling you to strengthen in order to increase your focus and intentional response to the pilot's every move?

DAY 20

MIGHT

*I arise today
through God's might to uphold me...*

Surely God is my help; the Lord is the one who sustains me (Psalm 54:4).

I'll be honest, this image of God's might is more challenging for me than it probably should be.

Human history has been plagued with the idea that "might makes right." People will do almost anything to gain power and keep it, no matter who they hurt or walk over in the process. As Lord Acton writes, "Power corrupts, and absolute power corrupts absolutely."[18] To some degree, we all want power and control.

I remember children's songs in church like "What a Mighty God We Serve," or "My God is so big, so strong and so mighty, there's nothing my God cannot do."

On one hand the idea that God is mightier and more powerful than any enemy we may face can be comforting, that is, so long as God is on our side. On the other hand, it is hard to imagine absolute power that does not corrupt. Absolute power and might is a frightening thought.

In Revelation, the saints of God sing out the song of Moses saying,

> Lord, who will not fear and glorify your name?
> For you alone are holy. All nations will come and worship before you, for your judgments have been revealed (Revelation 15:4).

Who would not fear the Lord, indeed? "The Lord, strong and mighty. The Lord mighty in battle" (Psalm 24:8). The King of Glory is King of Kings and Lord of Lords and no power or nation shall stand against our God.

Such imagery, though true, gives me pause. History has shown us time and time again that absolute power cannot

---

[18] "Lord Acton Quote Archive," Acton Institute, accessed October 17, 2019, https://acton.org/research/lord-acton-quote-archive.

go unchecked. It is dangerous. And yet we know God has no equal. Nothing can stand against the Lord.

The key difference between God's absolute power and corruptible human power is that God's might is perfectly balanced by God's unfailing love. We have the story in Genesis 18:16-33 where Abraham pleads with God on behalf of the people and God promises to relent for the sake of even 10 righteous people in the city. Regardless of the outcome, God does not relate to Abraham as some cosmic heartless monster out to destroy the world like so many other gods throughout history.

Unlike other gods, the God of Scripture is Love. God cannot exercise power and might in any way that does not reflect God's loving character.

Nearly every encounter a person has with God in Scripture pans out the same way. Consider the stories of Isaiah, Peter, Paul, and John in Revelation, among others. The person is overwhelmed by God's holiness, often falling on their face as though dead. God's first words in such terrifying moments almost always include the statement, "Do not fear."

In Isaiah 41, we find God's encouragement to Israel.

> "You are my servant, I have chosen you and not cast you off"; do not fear, for I am with you, do not be afraid, for I am your God; I will strengthen you, I will

help you, I will uphold you with my victorious right hand (Isaiah 41:9b-10).

God's might, rather than striking terror into our hearts, should fill us with hope and courage. God's righteous strong hand will uphold us. Because of God's might, we truly have nothing to fear.

Yet we must be careful, for unlike God, our sense of power often does lead to corruption. Centuries of ugly and violent religious history have shown us how easily we humans distort the power and might of God into a threat against our enemies, justifying countless wars in God's name and condemning all who disagree with us to the fires of hell. We must remember Jesus' call to love our enemies, and that God desires no one to perish but for all to come to repentance (Matthew 5:43-48, John 3:16-17). We must not seek to manipulate God's might for our own purposes. Our enemies are not God's enemies, for even they are beloved and bear the image of their Creator.

God's might will uphold us, but God's love must prevent us from using that might to tear down others. Perhaps the mightiest act in scripture was the restraint God showed at the cross by refusing to send down angel armies to destroy those who crucified God's beloved Son. Might is not the power to tear down or lord over others. The greatest might of all is the power to sacrifice everything for the sake of love.

Reflections:

What is your gut reaction to the thought of a "Mighty God"?

In what ways have you experienced God's might upholding you throughout your life?

How do you see God's power at work in sacrificial acts of love?

DAY 21

WISDOM

I arise today
through God's wisdom to guide me

One of my favorite 80's movies is "Short Circuit." As the robot, Number 5, increases in his own self-awareness, he begins to consume as much information as he can. "Input... Need Input," he says as he flies through the pages of every book in the house.[19]

Like Number 5, we as human beings have an insatiable thirst for new information. We want to be "in the know" about everything, and we are often unwilling to admit just

---

[19] John Badham, *Short Circuit* (Image Entertainment, 1986).

how much we don't know about so many things. We need input.

There is nothing wrong with acquiring knowledge. I personally place a high value on my education. The problem, however, is not our knowledge or lack of knowledge, but how we apply what knowledge we have. That is where wisdom comes in. As the old saying goes, "Knowledge may teach us that a tomato is a fruit, but wisdom tells us not to put it in a fruit salad or a smoothie."

Perhaps the most beautiful and yet sometimes frightening thing about wisdom is that it is no respecter of persons. It is possible for a child to say something wiser than a Nobel Prize winner. Wisdom does not depend on our level of education or how much knowledge we have. A person might have a photographic memory and store up more information than anyone else and still act foolishly. Likewise, a person who never went to school can be "wise beyond their years" in the way they treat others and in how they use whatever resources they have. Wisdom is all about our ability to rightly apply what we know, regardless of how much or how little knowledge we have.

I say it's a beautiful thing because anything that levels the playing field of our social hierarchies can result in greater humility, mutual respect, empathy and love. It is also frightening because those of us who have gained great knowledge in our lives tend to be proud of what we know.

Perhaps this is the reason wisdom is in such short supply. Where "knowledge is power," wisdom often brings humility which in our culture may be interpreted as weakness. Scripture tells us that all Wisdom comes from God and that it is freely available to anyone.

> If any of you lacks wisdom, you should ask God, who gives generously to all without finding fault, and it will be given to you (James 1:5, NIV).

In an age where false information masquerades as fact and truth is mistaken as fiction, wisdom is perhaps more crucial than ever. In the same way we gather much of our news through social media headlines or tweets with no substance or nuance, so often our knowledge of scripture is limited to the few verses or catchy "Christian" sayings we read on our Facebook or Instagram feeds.

Some people have greater access to knowledge than others. Some people can afford higher levels of education or greater connectivity to the "information highway," but everyone has equal access to Wisdom if we only ask.

What would happen if we asked God for wisdom as readily as we seek out and consume new information? Instead of striving to read the entire Bible in a year, for example, what would happen if we took just a few verses and meditated on them day and night to consider how they shape our everyday lives?

Here are just a few to consider:

- 1 John 4:7-11
- Mark 4:35-41
- Matthew 5:1-10
- Matthew 5:43-48
- Romans 12:1-2
- Psalm 23
- Galatians 5:22-26

Choose one of these passages, or another that God lays on your heart, and sit with it for an entire week without reading anything else. Read the immediate context before and after these verses, but beyond that, simply ask God each day to examine your heart and show you specific ways to better apply these passages in your day to day life. Ask God for wisdom as you read and meditate on the Word. Read it over and over again. Sit with the words in silence for a while. Jot down anything the Spirit of Wisdom may be speaking to your heart.

Wisdom is a slow process which is yet another reason we rarely ask for it. We want wisdom like we want patience… right now. Knowledge gives us the instant gratification we crave, but it is only a shadow of the Wisdom God desires for us.

> Woe to those who are wise in their own eyes and clever in their own sight (Isaiah 5:21, NIV).

Trust in the Lord with all your heart and lean not on your own understanding; in all your ways submit to him, and he will make your paths straight. Do not be wise in your own eyes; fear the Lord and shun evil (Proverbs 3:5-7, NIV).

So let us seek the wisdom of the Lord, for "the wisdom that comes from heaven is first of all pure; then peace-loving, considerate, submissive, full of mercy and good fruit, impartial and sincere" (James 3:17, NIV).

Reflections:

How do you see the relationship between knowledge and wisdom play out in your own life?

Have you every explicitly asked God for wisdom as you read the scriptures? What was that experience like?

Choose one of the passages from today's reflection, or another short passage of scripture God lays on your heart and sit with it for at least a week (longer if the Spirit leads).

One method to consider is the ancient practice of Lectio Divina. For a guide on this practice, visit https://www.contemplativeoutreach.org/lectio-divina.

Journal about the insights you gain and about your overall experience of reading scripture in this way.

DAY 22

GOD'S EYE

I arise today
through God's eye to look before me

In spite of this, you did not trust in the Lord your God, who went ahead of you on your journey, in fire by night and in a cloud by day, to search out places for you to camp and to show you the way you should go (Deuteronomy 1:32-33, NIV).

Deuteronomy 1 recalls the story of Israelite scouts who looked ahead to the land God promised but in seeing the inhabitants there, they turned back and grumbled against God for leading them into an impossible situation. God's eye looked before them even as they cried out from slavery in Egypt. God's eye saw a future filled with hope and blessing for all the world through this redeemed people. They could only see through the eyes of fear.

As we arise today through God's eye to look before us, two questions come to mind.

First, do we really trust that God's eye is looking out before us?

God set Israel free from Egypt and looked out for them day after day in the wilderness, providing for their every need. Still the people grumbled and did not trust that God was truly looking out for them. Over and over in Scripture we find people complaining that God has led them into a trap, that God has abandoned them, that God would not take care of them, that somehow God's way was not good enough. Even in the gospels, we find Jesus looking ahead through God's eyes at the suffering he would endure and his closest friend, Peter, challenges him.

> And Peter took him aside and began to rebuke him, saying, "God forbid it, Lord! This must never happen to you." But he turned and said to Peter, "Get behind me, Satan! You are a stumbling block to me; for you are setting your mind not on divine things but on human things" (Matthew 16:22-23).

God sees the path more clearly than any of us, but sometimes it is difficult to trust. Like the famous "Leap of Faith" scene in Indiana Jones and the Last Crusade, sometimes we can't even see the bridge God is asking us to cross.[20] We're not even sure there is anything there to step on. Where is God leading us?

That leads to our second question. Do we really want God's eye to look out before us, or would we rather just see for ourselves?

Have you ever played "Follow the Leader" with your eyes closed or blindfolded? It's a classic children's game in church to teach lessons about faith and listening to the Spirit. The goal is to go wherever the leader tells you to go, trusting that they won't lead you to walk into a wall or a chair. To make the game more challenging, everybody can shout out directions at once, so you must listen more carefully for the leader's voice to know which way to go in the midst of the chaos.

Honestly, I always hated those games. I don't think I've ever completed one without peeking. Sometimes I didn't trust the leader, but often, I didn't trust myself. What if I heard the direction wrong? What if he says left and he meant his left instead of mine? It's one thing for kids to wander blindly around a classroom bumping into one another, but what if you tried to do the same thing while driving, with only a voice over the phone to tell you when to turn, when to brake, etc. The stakes just got a lot higher

---

[20] Steven Spielberg, *Indiana Jones and the Last Crusade* (Paramount, 1989).

and I imagine even the most faithful among us would not take on such a challenge.

Yet that's often what it feels like to trust God's eyes instead of our own. When all we see ahead is fog, do we really want to trust that God can still see the way, or would we rather just camp out for a while until the fog clears and we can see for ourselves. In November 2017, I wrote a song called, "Through the Fog" about learning to see clearly when it feels like we can't see or feel anything at all. You can hear it on my website at the resource link below.[21]

Here's the irony. We naturally trust our own sight more than we trust what someone else sees, even if that someone is God. Yet whenever God's people in Scripture rely on their own sight, they almost always take a wrong turn. Why? Because their vision, like ours, is clouded. Our vision is blurred by sin, by doubts, by pain, and, most often, by fear. We never see as clearly as we think we do.

Maybe this is the reason Jesus tells the Pharisees, "If you were blind, you would not have sin. But now that you say, 'We see,' your sin remains" (John 9:41).

---

[21] "I Arise Today – Resources," Echo, https://www.craigsefa.org/arise/resources. Day 22.

Reflections:

How do you think you would score on a "spiritual vision test?" What "astigmatisms" keep you from seeing clearly? Fear... Doubt... Hurt... Sin... Something else?

Reflect on a time when you truly took a leap of faith and trusted God's leading, even when it looked absurd or impossible to you. What was the outcome?

Read the story of the blind man in John 9:1-41. Where do you find yourself in the story? Who do you most identify with? Why?

DAY 23

GOD'S EAR

*I arise today
through God's ear to hear me...*

Parents know the difference in a child's cries. They can tell when an infant truly needs something and when she is simply soothing herself to sleep. They can tell when a toddler is truly hurt and when he is just pretending. They know the difference between genuine screams and pitching a fit for attention or crying for not getting his or her way.

If we as human parents can understand these cries and know how to appropriately respond in so many different circumstances, God must certainly know how to respond to our cries. How many nights have we cried ourselves to sleep, not realizing God was listening patiently and prayerfully on the monitor, aware enough to respond if we truly needed while also giving us the space we needed as we learned to soothe ourselves? How many temper tantrums have we thrown thinking God didn't care when all the while, God was just waiting in the other room long enough for us to calm down and re-engage in the conversation? How often do we sound like the child begging to "be blessed" with every piece of candy or toy in the store?

Like earthly parents, God hears all our cries. God listens. God waits patiently, just like the father of the prodigal son (Luke 15:11-32). Rather than forcing us to stay at the table kicking and screaming through the entire meal, God lets us get it out of our system and reminds us through the Holy Spirit that we are welcome back whenever we are ready.

If we're honest, there are simply times when children don't know how to talk to their parents. Children are not always sure that parents will understand or even care about whatever feels so overwhelming in their little lives. We often wonder the same thing about God. Does God even want me around? Is God listening anymore? Have I wandered too far away for God to hear me?

Meanwhile, the moment we get tired in the waiting, God's Spirit is right alongside helping us along. If we don't know how or what to pray, it doesn't matter. He does our praying in and for us, making prayer out of our wordless sighs, our aching groans. He knows us far better than we know ourselves, knows our pregnant condition, and keeps us present before God. That's why we can be so sure that every detail in our lives of love for God is worked into something good (Romans 8:26-28, MSG).

Romans 8:28 is often used to explain how everything in life is part of some Divine plan to do good for us, but the larger context shows that this is a passage about God hearing our cries. God even understands those times when we just need to scream and pitch a fit, when we don't know how to articulate what we really need.

The Spirit speaks for us, "making prayer out of our wordless sighs and our aching groans, for God knows us far better than we know ourselves and… the Spirit keeps us present before God." That's why Paul says God is working everything out for good.

God doesn't fix every problem in our lives, but God listens to us and even prays for us through every circumstance. When we feel like nobody is listening, we arise today trusting that God is a God who hears (Psalm 66:19, 1 John 5:14-15).

Shout

Scream

Laugh

Cry

Argue

Praise

Question

Whisper

Be Silent

Whatever you feel,
whatever you need to express,
do it openly before God.

God hears.

Reflections:

Reflect on a time (perhaps even now) when it seems like your prayers are not getting through to God.

How do you feel about the idea that the Spirit is praying for you even when you don't have the words? How might this change the way you pray and the way you experience God's presence with you?

Pray along with Solomon as he dedicates the Temple in 2 Chronicles 6 found on the next page.

2 Chronicles 6:18-21 (The Message)

Can it be that God will actually move into our neighborhood? Why, the cosmos itself isn't large enough to give you breathing room, let alone this Temple I've built. Even so, I'm bold to ask: Pay attention to these my prayers, both intercessory and personal, O God, my God. Listen to my prayers, energetic and devout, that I'm setting before you right now. Keep your eyes open to this Temple day and night, this place you promised to dignify with your Name. And listen to the prayers that I pray in this place. And listen to your people Israel when they pray at this place.

Listen from your home in heaven, and when you hear, forgive.

Take some time to worship with the song, "Hear us from Heaven" from New Life Worship.[22]

Envision God reaching out to invite you closer into his loving presence and know that you are being heard.

---

[22] New Life Worship, *Hear Us From Heaven* (Integrity Music, 2014). Video available at "I Arise Today – Resources," Echo, https://www.craigsefa.org/arise/resources. Day 23.

DAY 24

GOD'S WORD

*I arise today
through God's word to speak for me*

Clearly we want God's word to hold a central place in our lives, speaking to hearts and guiding us through whatever circumstances we may face. I am struck today, however, by what this line does not say about God's word.

It does not say: "God's word to be *read* by me"

Of course we must read and study and meditate on God's word, but I think the writer of this prayer is getting at something a bit deeper. We must remember that the

Word became flesh, not text. Even the pages of Scripture cannot fully contain the Living and breathing Word of God, incarnate in the person of Jesus our Lord. We may find God's word primarily in the Bible, but reading the Bible alone is not enough. If we are not careful, the Bible itself may become an idol. We must not merely read the word with our eyes and process it with our minds. Rather, we must embody the Word of God in our hearts and lives. Since it is God's word which breathed life into us, every breath we take and every word we speak should flow forth from the Living Presence of God's word dwelling within us.

It does not say: "God's word to be ***spoken*** by me"

We are very good at quoting scripture verses when they suit our purposes. We often use them as ammunition in our political battles or to condemn someone for a behavior we do not like. Yes, we are to proclaim the words of Scripture and preach the Good News of Christ wherever we are, but there is a big difference between "speaking the words" and having the word speak *for* us.

In speaking the words, we tend to filter them through our own lens, our own stories and our own system of beliefs or ideologies. These lenses are shaped by our families, our culture, our denominations, and countless other influences which can easily manipulate the word for their own purposes. Our lens is not always bad, but we must be aware that we all interpret scripture, and life, from a specific worldview. Our worldview may not be the same as someone else's, which often leads to differing interpretations. They are not always wrong. We are not always right. Sometimes, by God's grace, we may both be right, from different perspectives and in different circumstances.

God's word may indeed be a sword, but it is not ours to wield. When we allow God's word to speak for us, we give up our agendas and remove our lenses so that others may encounter the Living Word for themselves. As Philip told Nathanael about Jesus, "Come and see" (John 1:46). The world doesn't need our "opinions" about God's word. They simply need to "come and see" God's Living Word for themselves. So do we. #unfiltered.

It does not even say: "God's word to *speak to* me"

God's word speaks to us in many ways, but again, I think the prayer is getting at something a bit deeper. Often when we go to Scripture, we are looking to get "a word from God." Even better if that word just happens to be a word for someone else and not for me, especially if the word challenges my beliefs or behaviors. My preaching professor, Dr. Ellsworth Kalas, used to say that "If you don't know a passage or a topic well enough to sit down at a kitchen table and have a conversation about it, you do not yet know it well enough to preach." This was his way of teaching us to preach without notes, as though we are simply having a conversation with the congregation.

I think this perspective is valuable for all of us. God does not speak the word to us during times of devotional reading and then allow us to close the book and walk away until next time. Instead, God's word goes with us. It doesn't just speak to us, but it becomes a part of us. The rhythms and melodies of Scripture become part of our everyday actions and conversation, not because we are always trying to quote what we read or what God spoke to us in our quiet time, but because they have become a part of us, like that song we can't stop humming because it is stuck in our heads. "What comes out of the mouth proceeds from the heart," Jesus says (Matthew 15:18). Likewise, James writes:

> With the tongue we praise our Lord and Father, and with it we curse human beings, who have been made in God's likeness. Out of the same mouth come praise and cursing. My brothers and sisters, this should not be. Can both fresh water and saltwater flow from the same spring? (James 3:9-11, NIV).

If God's word is to speak "for us" and not merely "to us", it must first become a part of us. It is Living Water that gushes from within us; the source of every word we speak. As we arise today, let us not seek to speak for God, but rather allow God's word to speak for us.

Reflections:

Do my words sound like something Jesus would say? What specific words of Jesus are reflected in my everyday speech?

What lenses or filters influence my understanding of God's word? How might I intentionally see God's word through the lens of another so that together, our eyes may be opened even more?

Reflect on a circumstance when you could feel God's word bubbling up from your heart like a fresh-water spring and you knew it was God, not you, who was speaking life into that situation.

DAY 25

GOD'S HAND

I arise today
through God's hand to guard me

My sheep listen to my voice; I know them, and they follow me. I give them eternal life, and they shall never perish; no one will snatch them out of my hand. My Father, who has given them to me, is greater than all; no one can snatch them out of my Father's hand. I and the Father are one" (John 10:27-29).

I will never forget an illustration I heard once from a Southern Baptist evangelist about God's hand. He was preaching on this text from John 10 where Jesus promises that no one can "snatch his sheep out of his Father's hand."

> Even if the Devil managed to pry open the all-powerful grip of God's hand, he would still have to swim through the blood of Jesus, and even then he would still have to unravel the Holy Spirit from our heart and soul, and by the time the Devil did all of that you would end up with a saved devil.

Looking back, I recognize the illustration is far from perfect, but I must give it credit for being thoroughly Trinitarian, recognizing the power of Father, Son, and Holy Spirit in our salvation and in guarding our lives from the snares of temptation. It also reminds us, as the classic song says, that God indeed has "You and me brother, in his hands. You and me sister, in his hands. He's got the whole world in his hands."[23]

Scripture tells us that God's strong right hand will uphold us and that God will guard us like the shepherd guards his sheep so that we will not be led astray.

I find it interesting that in back to back lines of this prayer we see first God's hand guarding us and then God's shield protecting us. Yes, these are parallel images that have many similarities, but as with our distinction between "rock" and "earth" earlier in the prayer, it is worth

---

[23] Traditional African American Spiritual

exploring the nuances here. We will come back to the image of God's shield tomorrow, but at first glance a shield seems preferable to a hand when it comes to guarding us. A shield is more resilient to attack. A shield will not bleed when struck by the arrows of enemy archers. I'm reminded of a clip from Tim Hawkins about the way Christians pray for a "hedge of protection."

> A hedge, huh? I don't mean to complain, but is that really the best you can do? How about praying a thick cement wall with some razor wire on top of that bad boy? A hedge of protection sounds like it is one good pair of clippers away from being removed — and I'm sure the devil's got a pair of those lying around the old Sheol Shed.[24]

Indeed, a shield does sound stronger than a hedge or a hand, but there is something more personal about a hand. Rather than a scene of battle with shields and barricades, God's hand calls to mind a more relational and even emotional image.

To guard with one's hand is a more loving gesture than simply locking someone in a safe room. It requires direct presence. God's hand to guard us implies that God is right there with us, in person. God does not sit in some distant office watching over us through closed circuit

---

[24] "Hedge of Protection... Prayer Can Be a Funny Thing," Tim Hawkins. Video available at "I Arise Today – Resources," Echo, https://www.craigsefa.org/arise/resources. Day 25.

security cameras. God chooses to "get his hands dirty" in the mess of our everyday lives.

I picture the image of a mother in the car reaching out her hand instinctively to guard her child in the passenger seat after a sudden stop or perhaps a father catching a younger child before he or she runs into the street. Whereas a shield protects from external attack, the loving hand of a parent guards us by holding us back. The parent's hand keeps us from hitting our head on the dashboard or from running headlong into traffic. The hand is a warning that tells us there is danger ahead.

It may be true that nothing can pry us out of God's hand, or as Paul puts it, that nothing can separate us from God's love (Romans 8:38). For some, however, the idea of being in God's grasp calls to mind images of being smothered by an overprotective or even abusive parent. We might instead take comfort in the image of an open hand, outstretched in front of us as a warning so that we will stop and become more aware of the dangers and temptations in our path.

Reflections:

What image does the idea of God's hand call to your imagination?

Reflect on a time when you felt smothered by God's hand. Looking back, how do you see God at work in that instance?

How does it feel to imagine God's hand as a warning or a safeguard keeping you from stepping into harm or wandering astray? What emotions does that image stir in your heart? How might you respond to the presence of God's loving hand in your life?

DAY 26

GOD'S SHIELD

*I arise today
through God's shield to protect me*

The Lord is my strength and my shield;
   in him my heart trusts;
so I am helped, and my heart exults,
   and with my song I give thanks to him (Psalm 28:7).

As we saw on Day 8, God promises Abraham a great reward (Genesis 15:1). The most literal translation of the Hebrew here reads: "I am a shield to you, your very great reward."

God is not providing Abraham with some external source

of protection or reward. God is Abraham's shield and great reward. In Ephesians 6:16, Paul describes the "shield of faith, with which we can extinguish all the flaming arrows of the evil one." The key here lies in the object of our faith. What or who do we trust for our security?

As humans, we regularly put our faith in any number of things to provide safety and security in our lives. We trust in our own strength. We trust in job security, education, healthcare, retirement funds, our military or police, even our guns. Our currency says, "In God We Trust" but as some have said, a more accurate statement may be "In THIS god we trust," because in many cases money itself has become our shield and our god.

On Sundays we go to church to proclaim our trust in God, but the rest of the week we spend building bigger and stronger safety nets to protect us from any worst-case scenario. We build our nets so wide that it almost wouldn't matter if God was there for us or not. Like rebellious adolescents, we essentially say, "I can take care of myself." It's almost as if, underneath it all, we are afraid that God might not come through and we need a backup plan. If we truly believe God is the perfect shield, why do we need to protect ourselves so well?

We talk a great deal about security, safety and protection, but in truth, we spend most of lives living in fear. Fear is not the absence of faith. Fear is putting our faith in the wrong things, in things that cannot truly save us.

We have insurance, security systems, weapons and defenses of all kinds. We have law enforcement and neighborhood watches to keep the streets safe. We have shelters that are more than capable of weathering almost any storm. Yet in all of this, we are still afraid. In fact, the industries who produce all the "shields" we use to protect ourselves actually tell us to be afraid.

Fear makes a wonderful marketing strategy. If you want to sell a warranty, you must make the customer afraid that the product may break within a certain amount of time. If you want to sell a home security system, you must convince them their neighborhood is not safe. The great irony here is that all the people who make a fortune trying to "protect us" are the very ones convincing us that we need protection in the first place.

God is different. God doesn't promise safety and security the same way an insurance company or a gun dealer might. God doesn't promise that nothing bad will ever happen.

In almost every encounter with humanity, God's first words are "Do not be afraid."

In fact, this is exactly how God begins with Abraham. "*Do not be afraid*, Abram. I am your shield, your very great reward" (Genesis 15:1, NIV).

Reflections:

What are you most afraid of?

What safety nets do you have in place to protect yourself? How much time, energy and resources do you invest in these compared to what you invest in your relationship with God?

Where have you seen God's protection in your life?

DAY 27

GOD'S HOST

*I arise today
through God's host to save me*

Over the next few days we will explore specific ways God's host saves us, but for now, let's take a few moments to ask, what exactly is "God's host?"

This is not a term we hear very often but it has a rich tradition Scripture and church history.

The term "heavenly host" in scripture often refers to angels or "angel armies" (Psalm 148:2, 1 Kings 22:19, Luke 2:13-14). The problem with angels is we don't always recognize them when we see them. The writer of Hebrews says, "Do not neglect to show hospitality to strangers, for by doing that some have entertained angels without knowing it" (Hebrews 13:2). When the three visitors came to announce the birth of Isaac to Abraham and Sarah, Abraham welcomed them and showed them hospitality as strangers in his midst (Genesis 18:1-22). They appeared as ordinary men. Had Abraham neglected to show hospitality, we do not know if they would have stuck around to deliver the message.

Similarly, Jesus himself walked with the disciples on the road to Emmaus, but they did not recognize him (Luke 24:13-35). He was going to continue on his way until they showed hospitality by inviting him to stay for dinner. In the breaking of bread at the table their eyes were opened to the presence of God. Throughout scripture we find that recognizing the presence of God's host, or even of God's personal and immediate presence, often begins with an act of hospitality toward a stranger.

How often have we missed the presence of God's host among us because we ignored the stranger in our midst?

The "heavenly host" also expands beyond angelic beings to include all of God's creation, for God is enthroned in the heavens and "the earth is God's footstool" (Isaiah 66:1). The point here is not that God treats us as lowly beings to be stepped upon like a footstool. Rather it is to say the entire created order is just that, something created or made by God. When the Psalmist declares, "Praise Him, sun and moon; Praise Him, all you shining stars!" we are reminded that even the sun and moon and stars bow before God (Psalm 148:3). In Jeremiah 31:35 the prophet explicitly refers to the God who created these celestial bodies as the Lord of Hosts, implying in part that the sun, moon and stars may be among God's host. Zephaniah 1:5 refers to these as the "starry host." Rather than being gods themselves, as so many ancient people believed, they serve the purposes of the God who made them (Deuteronomy 4:19).

In some cases, even human beings can serve as God's host. Consider 1 Samuel 7:45 where the "Lord of Hosts" commands Israel's armies in battle. This is not to say that any human army is the Lord's host. Throughout the Old Testament the nation of Israel was set apart as the kingdom of God. God fought with them and for them unlike any other nation throughout history.

No matter how broadly or narrowly we define the heavenly host, we can say two things for certain. First, the host of God is many… myriad upon myriad. The word host literally means multitude and was often used in the ancient world to refer to massive and intimidating armies. Whether in the form of angels, celestial bodies, or even human beings called for a particular purpose, the host of God is many.

Host also hearkens us back to the image of hospitality. To be a good host is to show hospitality to others. The second thing we know of the heavenly host is how they extend hospitality to welcome God's presence. As hosts, they function as servants of the Most High God. Perhaps this is why some parts of the church refer to the bread in the Eucharist as the "Host", for in this ordinary bread, the holy mystery of God's presence is "hosted" or made welcome, so that God may enter into our bodies and make us the body of Christ for the sake of the world.

May we also serve as hosts of the Lord, always extending hospitality both to the Holy Spirit and to the strangers among us, so that God's presence may always be welcome in our midst.

Reflections:

How do you understand the idea of God's host?

What new insights is the Spirit speaking to you about the role of God's hosts in your life?

Reflect on a time when God clearly showed up in an act of genuine hospitality toward a stranger.

DAY 28

SNARES OF DEVILS

*I arise today
through God's host to save me
from snares of devils...*

"I arise today through God's host to save me from snares of devils, from temptation of vices, and from everyone who shall wish me ill, afar and near."

These next three lines of our prayer fit nicely together. They essentially summarize what we have been talking about over the past few days, that God guards, protects, and saves us. Plain and simple.

It is one thing, however, to say that God saves, and quite

another to wrestle with those things from which we need saving. In general, we feel pretty good about ourselves. Many people don't think they need saving. Even Christians, who believe in Jesus to forgive their sins and save them for heaven, do not always recognize that God's saving work goes much deeper than handing out golden tickets for Saint Peter to collect at the pearly gates.

Patrick's prayer says specifically that God's host saves us from the snares of devils, from temptation of vices, and from everyone who shall wish me ill, afar and near.

Today, let's focus on those "snares of devils."

In the C.S. Lewis classic, Screwtape Letters, uncle Screwtape trains his nephew on how to be more effective as a demon leading his "patient" away from God. In one letter, Screwtape writes:

> Indeed, the safest road to Hell is the gradual one--the gentle slope, soft underfoot, without sudden turnings, without milestones, without signposts... Your affectionate uncle, Screwtape.[25]

Snares are generally hidden. If they were clearly marked, they would not be snares. No one willingly walks into a trap. We often don't realize that we have been caught by a snare. Last spring my daughter and I took a "Lobster

---

[25] C. S Lewis, *The Screwtape Letters* (New York, NY: Simon & Schuster, 1982).; 54.

Boat" cruise off the coast of Portland, Maine. As we pulled up the traps, I realized the genius of their design. The lobsters can easily crawl in to get the bait without noticing, but they cannot get out. There is plenty of room in the trap for them to crawl around. They can live comfortably in their cage without realizing anything is wrong until they suddenly find themselves out of the water.

I doubt the lobster has much awareness of such details, but as humans we often find ourselves resting comfortably in traps without knowing it. Paul warns Timothy of such snares when he says:

> Run away from infantile indulgence. Run after mature righteousness—faith, love, peace—joining those who are in honest and serious prayer before God. Refuse to get involved in inane discussions; they always end up in fights. God's servant must not be argumentative, but a gentle listener and a teacher who keeps cool, working firmly but patiently with those who refuse to obey. You never know how or when God might sober them up with a change of heart and a turning to the truth, *enabling them to escape the Devil's trap* [or snare], where they are caught and held captive, forced to run his errands (2 Timothy 2:22-26, MSG).

In this passage, Paul teaches Timothy how to help people escape the Devil's trap. What strikes me is the reference to "inane discussions that end up in fights" and the call not to be argumentative, even with those who "refuse to obey." We always want to win the argument, and we are even more determined because we believe that "being right" is a matter of eternal life or death, heaven or hell. Yet Paul implies that such methods will only drive others away. "You never know," he says, "when God may change their heart." The method God uses to change hearts and free people from snares will not be our arguments, but our gentleness, patience, and love.

We may not visibly stumble into the Devil's fiery pit, but how often have we found ourselves falling deeper and deeper into the rabbit hole of our twisted logic and desperation to convince everyone else how right we are and how wrong they are? Are we more concerned about loving others or about winning them over to our way of thinking? This argumentative way of being is increasingly common among Christians, but we must call it what it is, a snare of the devil and a trap we don't even realize we have entered.

Perhaps it is "we", not "them", who need to pray for a change of heart, that we might escape the snares that have so subtly trapped us in lives and purposes that are far too small.

Reflections:

What kinds of snares have distracted you from God throughout your life?

How have you experienced the futility of arguments?

What truth is God speaking to you that may help you escape the snares that keep you feeling stuck or trapped?

DAY 29

TEMPTATION OF VICES

I arise today
through God's host to save me
from temptation of vices

No temptation has overtaken you except what is common to mankind. And God is faithful; he will not let you be tempted beyond what you can bear. But when you are tempted, he will also provide a way out so that you can endure it (1 Corinthians 10:13, NIV).

Paul does not say that we will never be overwhelmed by difficult circumstances or suffering. He does say we will not be overcome by temptation. When we talk about salvation we often think of God's forgiveness and mercy.

We imagine being saved "from the fires of hell" by the grace of Jesus given freely through the sacrifice of his blood. While this is true, salvation involves more than a "free ticket" to heaven. God not only saves us from the eternal punishment for sin, but from the power of sin. We read throughout the New Testament that in Christ we are new creations, that we are no longer slaves to sin, and that God gives us the strength to resist temptation in any form (2 Corinthians 5:17; Romans 6, 8, and 12; Ephesians 6:10-12; Galatians 2:20; James 4:7; etc.).

Some people participate in various recovery programs because of addictions and other such vices that have taken a significant and painful toll on their lives. For others, the temptation of vices is not so clear. A vice doesn't have to be an extremely harmful addiction. It may be a habitual failing or shortcoming which we easily overlook because, after all, we are only human. Just because we do not engage in what we might consider moral depravity or wickedness does not mean our lives are free of faults and even idols. No matter how big or small, vices always turn our attention away from God.

I confess it is much easier in the morning to open my e-mail or social media feed than to set aside intentional time for prayer before work. Would I rather relax in the evening with a good TV show to unwind or sit down with my journal and the Daily Examen to reflect on how I responded or failed to respond to God's presence throughout the day? Again, I think the answer is obvious.

Vices are not always "bad things." That is precisely what makes them so tempting. Merriam Webster's dictionary notes that vices may be trivial, using the example, "suffering from the vice of curiosity." Curiosity may indeed be a strength until it leads us into places we don't belong. It's not the severity or immorality of the vice that makes it so harmful. It's the habitual way in which such vices, no matter how small, consume our lives and distract us from that which is most important.

Eugene Peterson paraphrases Paul this way when he talks about the failures of God's children throughout the Hebrew Scriptures:

> These are all warning markers—danger! — in our history books, written down so that we don't repeat their mistakes. Our positions in the story are parallel—they at the beginning, we at the end—and we are just as capable of messing it up as they were. Don't be so naive and self-confident. You're not exempt. You could fall flat on your face as easily as anyone else. Forget about self-confidence; it's useless. Cultivate God-confidence (1 Corinthians 10:11-12, MSG).

The NIV translates verse 12 this way:

> So, if you think you are standing firm, be careful that you don't fall!

Reflections:

Name the three most common temptations that distract you from keeping God central in your life.

How have you tried to be self-reliant rather than relying on God to overcome these vices?

What steps will you take to daily put yourself in the path of God's grace so that you may have the strength to resist such temptations?

DAY 30

EVERYONE WHO SHALL WISH ME ILL

*I arise today
through God's host to save me
from everyone who shall wish me ill, afar or near*

Paranoia and fear blaze through our culture like a raging forest fire. Everywhere we turn it seems there is someone who wishes us ill, both far and near. They may be as distant as refugees at the border or politicians in Washington or as close as the person in the next pew in church or across the dinner table in our home. Such fears are often rooted in our perceptions rather than in real threats to our being. The people we are most certain are "out to get us" likely don't view us as significant enough to bother with. In some ways, our fear of being harmed flows out of our own sense of pride and our inclination to think of ourselves more highly than we ought.

I once met a family who had turned their trailer home on a small rural street into a bunker with an arsenal of assault weapons lined up along hatches cut in the outside wall facing the street. The father said when the terrorists came marching through town to mutilate his daughters and granddaughters that they wouldn't get anywhere near his house. Clearly a major terrorist organization from halfway around the globe would not be interested in this tiny little rural crossroads in the middle of nowhere, but the perception made this family feel like they were prepared to be the saviors of their community. It was as much a delusion of grandeur as it was a delusion of terror that did not actually pose an imminent threat.

It is true that we have enemies. St. Patrick spent his childhood in slavery and in his world the threat of death was a real possibility. This portion of the prayer may be particularly valuable for those who are serving in war or on the front lines of local law enforcement or security. It may echo the prayers of powerful people who have made many enemies in their lives. It may even be a prayer on the lips of terrorists or drug lords who are always looking over their shoulder even though they have put themselves in that situation.

For most of us, however, God must first save us from our illusion that we are a central target to whoever we see as enemies. What if being saved from our enemies involves being reconciled with our enemies through love and forgiveness? An enemy turned friend through the love of Christ is no longer a threat. Maybe, just maybe, Jesus was onto something when he said:

> You have heard that it was said, 'You shall love your neighbor and hate your enemy.' But I say to you, love your enemies and pray for those who persecute you (Matthew 5:43-44).

I don't want to diminish in any way that there are some who truly do need salvation from dangerous situations. For those suffering from abuse, domestic violence, human trafficking, or other forms of intentional harm, this prayer is for you. May God's host indeed save you from all who wish you ill, afar and near, and may God place in your paths people who will stand with you against such evil.

If you are one, however, who tends to see enemies everywhere you look, every time you turn on the news, or every time you see someone who looks or thinks differently than you, maybe God wants to save you from your own fear and paranoia. Maybe God is inviting you to turn an enemy into a friend. Maybe, just maybe, hate and fear could be defeated by the power of love. Could it be that we are truly our own worst enemies?

Reflections:

Who is it that you feel you need saving from? Is the threat legitimate or perceived? If the threat is legitimate, who might God have placed in your path to help?

What triggers your fears or your feelings of being threatened? What steps will you take to listen more to the voice of God than the voices of fear in our world?

Pray for an "enemy" - by name. If you do not know someone personally, find someone in a news story who you might consider to be "against you" or your beliefs and pray for him or her. Perhaps a criminal, a terrorist, a politician from "the other party," etc. Reflect on how God may be changing your view of them as you pray and how God may be calling you to respond.

DAY 31

I SUMMON TODAY

> I summon today
> all these powers between me and those evils,
> against every cruel and merciless power
> that may oppose my body and soul

"I summon today…"

In this new stanza, the Breastplate Prayer moves us toward a summary or collection of everything we have prayed so far, inviting us to claim "all these powers" as our own. We ask God to stand between us and every evil, cruel or merciless power that may oppose our bodies and souls.

What are "these powers" that we may summon or call upon so boldly? Such a small word, "these", draws our attention back to the mighty strength of Triune God made manifest in countless ways.

Today we not only arise in, but we actively summon strength, obedience, service, hope, prayers, predictions, preaching, faith, innocence, righteous deeds, light, radiance, splendor, speed, swiftness, depth, stability, firmness, might, wisdom, God's eye, God's ear, God's word, God's hand, God's shield, and God's host.

Talk about calling down angel armies. In his discussion of our suffering and weakness in Romans 8, Paul writes,

> What, then, shall we say in response to these things? If God is for us, who can be against us? He who did not spare his own Son, but gave him up for us all—how will he not also, along with him, graciously give us all things? (Romans 8:31-32, NIV).

Indeed, if God freely gave up the life of his own son for our redemption, is there anything God would withhold? We not only arise with an awareness of these truths, but we boldly summon these powers in prayer so that we might stand against the forces of evil in our world.

We don't simply believe God will strengthen us, hear us, or protect us. We actively call upon God to step in and intervene in our lives with all these powers at God's disposal.

This is not a "name it, claim it" kind of theology. We are not saying that in summoning these powers we will be spared from all pain or suffering in our lives. We are not claiming a guaranteed victory over all the things that stand in our way. It may be, in fact, that some things which stand in our way are necessary for our own spiritual growth and humility.

All these powers, however, give us strength, hope and wisdom through whatever we face in life. God also calls us to summon these powers on behalf of others who suffer oppression in many forms, that we may stand in the gap for them as Moses does when he pleads for the people of Israel (Exodus 32-33).

The remainder of this stanza unpacks the nature of the various evils which oppose us. For now, take some time to read back through the entire prayer written out at the beginning of this book. As you slowly read each line, reflect on these gifts of strength and power which God so freely offers.

Reflections:

As you reflect on the list of powers throughout this prayer, which one do you need to summon most today and why?

What, if any, differences do you see between "arising" in these powers and actually "summoning" them to stand between you and evil?

Which of these powers may God be calling you to summon on behalf of someone else in your life and how will you do that this week?

DAY 32

AGAINST EVERY KNOWLEDGE THAT CORRUPTS

I summon today all these powers
against incantations of false prophets,
against black laws of pagandom,
against false laws of heretics,
against craft of idolatry,
against spells of witches and smiths and wizards,
against every knowledge that corrupts
man's body and soul

I must confess, at first glance I feel like I just stepped into the Middle Ages or stumbled onto Platform 9 3/4 into the

Wizarding World of Harry Potter.[26] Incantations, black laws, spells, and the like in our day tend to remain safely tucked away in fantasy novels, movies, or Renaissance Festivals. So why not just include these specific and seemingly outdated examples of evil in our previous section so we could gloss over them and move on with something more relevant?

Believe me, I thought about it.

In fact, making this separation ultimately resulted in a 41-day series rather than my intended 40-day journey. What concerns me, however, is that in reading any ancient work it is easy to gloss over things which at first glance seem irrelevant to us. If we're not careful, we can do the same with parts of Scripture we struggle to understand. And so, I pause today with this difficult stanza to practice the discipline of discovering the timeless Holy Spirit inspired truths within even the most distant writings of the Saints who have gone before us.

For me, the timeless word that strikes at the heart is "knowledge." "...Against every knowledge that corrupts man's body and soul."

These examples are forms of knowledge in Patrick's world, even if they are what we might consider less than scientific or rational.

---

[26] J. K Rowling and Mary GrandPré, *Harry Potter: The Complete Series*, 2008.

Paul writes to the church at Corinth,

> Not many of you were wise by human standards; not many were influential; not many were of noble birth. But God chose the foolish things of the world to shame the wise; God chose the weak things of the world to shame the strong (1 Corinthians 1:26b-27, NIV).

Just a few verses earlier in 1:18, he declares that "the cross is foolishness to those who are perishing."

This issue of knowledge and evil creates a very fine line we must walk in step with the Spirit. On one hand, we must be careful what kinds of knowledge we assume will corrupt us. Both Galileo and Copernicus were deemed heretics by the church and yet both are held in high regard today for their scientific discoveries. We no longer condemn the belief that the earth revolves around the sun as a contradiction of Scripture. We recognize that the Biblical writers described creation as they understood it. We also know that their purpose in writing was theological rather than scientific or historical in a strict modern sense. Christians today continue to hurt the church's witness when we declare things as heretical that are often simply matters of opinion or increased awareness and understandings of reality.

On the other hand, there are certainly heretical, idolatrous and pagan teachings which do corrupt our bodies and souls. Often these teachings find their way into the church in benign ways. Our theology of heaven or the return of Christ, for example, is often distorted in such a way that we fail to be good stewards of creation as God commanded because we assume it will all be destroyed. Our understanding of God's blessings and grace has led us to mistreat countless groups throughout history who we assume God has not blessed in the same way those of us who live with privilege understand blessings.

What if the greater danger today is not the knowledge of pagan ways, but the knowledge we think we have of God's word that has been so distorted by our own cultural values that we are no longer recognizable as a "people of the Book."

Let us not forget that those with the greatest religious knowledge in the gospels are condemned by Jesus as those who "strain out a gnat while swallowing a camel" (Matthew 23:24). Knowledge is not inherently good or evil, pagan or holy, secular or sacred. All knowledge may be interpreted and used for good or for evil. Let us weigh and evaluate carefully our sources of knowledge, but even more, let us be wise that we do not use our knowledge in ways that might corrupt our bodies and souls.

Reflections:

What first impressions did you have in reading the section of St. Patrick's prayer?

In what ways do you see this admonition to summon God's strength against these evils as relevant and applicable for you today?

How might God be inviting you to become more discerning in your sources and application of knowledge?

DAY 33

POISON, BURNING, DROWNING & WOUNDING

> Christ to shield me today
> against poison, against burning,
> against drowning, against wounding,
> so that there may come to me
> an abundance of reward

The Breastplate prayer, while often used in the mornings as a way of arising each day in the light of Christ's glory, is primarily a prayer of protection. In the previous lines, we asked God to protect us from the invisible powers of evil. Now we turn to far more tangible concerns; poison, burning, drowning, and wounding.

We must again admit to some cultural barriers in fully applying this prayer, as things like poison and burning do not generally pose a threat to us. On the other hand, there are ways that each of these threats still show up in our supposedly "more civilized culture." Let us consider each threat and what it might mean for us today.

Against poison…

While most of us do not need a royal food taster to make sure our enemies do not poison us, we still face poison in many forms. People struggle with the more obvious poisons of alcohol or drugs, especially given the present opioid crisis. In truth, any addictive behavior can become like a poison to our bodies and souls. Sin, in any form, eats away at our souls like a poison that destroys us from the inside out. I was once part of an accountability group where we regularly prayed, "Lord, make my sin taste like the poison it truly is." It was a way of remembering that even those seemingly small or insignificant acts of selfish desire would eventually consume us, perhaps more than some major moral failing.

Against burning…

Burning is a little tougher. The spiritual parallel is not as clear. Though some families lose everything in house fires and other similar disasters, I don't know anyone who faces the threat of being burned at the stake. In some ways, however, our corporate sin of greed and selfishness is "burning the earth" as we continue to burn fossil fuels and resist movements toward cleaner energy sources. We are doing harm to our environment and to future generations who will suffer the increasing effects. This is not the place for a political argument about climate change but suffice it to say that caring for God's creation is first a social, a moral, and a spiritual issue. Politics distract us from our God-given responsibilities as stewards and caregivers of the earth. The "burning of the earth" through global warming due to our own neglect, apathy and even abuse of natural resources inordinately impacts the poor and those who are unable to escape or do not have the infrastructure to withstand the "natural disasters" that are increasing in frequency and intensity at an alarming rate. (For more on the moral and ethical dimensions of climate change, check out the TED Talks by Katharine Hayhoe, "What if Climate Change is Real" and "The most important thing we can do to fight climate change: talk about it").[27]

---

[27] "What If Climate Change Is Real? | Katharine Hayhoe | TEDxTexasTechUniversity - YouTube," accessed October 17, 2019, https://www.youtube.com/watch?v=PtrYNGs9oRM; Katharine Hayhoe, *The Most Important Thing You Can Do to Fight Climate Change: Talk about It*, accessed October 17, 2019, https://www.ted.com/talks/katharine_hayhoe_the_most_important_thing_you_can_do_to_fight_climate_change_talk_about_it.

Videos and other resource links available at "I Arise Today – Resources," Echo, https://www.craigsefa.org/arise/resources. Day 33.

Against drowning…

There are certainly parallels between drowning and the climate change issues I mentioned above. Science has shown without question that as glaciers melt, sea levels continue to rise and coastal regions throughout the world are suffering disastrous consequences. There are of course spiritual dimensions to this danger as well. The Good News Translation of Psalm 38:4 says, "I am drowning in the flood of my sins; they are a burden too heavy to bear."[28] We do not need a cataclysmic weather event like Noah's flood to take seriously the ways our sin, both individual and as a society, can easily overwhelm us.

Against wounding…

Wounding comes in all forms. We pray for protection against physical harm. We must also take seriously the ways our hearts our wounded. As the saying goes, "hurt people hurt people." In other words, if we do not deal with our wounds or hurt, whether emotional, physical, spiritual, mental or in any other form, we will inevitably wound or hurt others out of a sense of self-preservation. Many of those we condemn for doing harm to others have been so deeply wounded themselves that they react violently out of utter desperation and hopelessness. We

---

[28] "Psalm 38:4 GNT - I Am Drowning in the Flood of My Sins; - Bible Gateway," accessed November 7, 2019, https://www.biblegateway.com/passage/?search=psalm+38%3A4&version=GNT.

must consistently pray to protect our hearts and souls from being wounded and perhaps even more, we must pray against the ways we wound or inflict harm upon others, no matter how innocent or unintentional.

Reflections:

Of the four dangers (poison, burning, drowning, wounding), which one resonates the most with you and why?

What other ways can you see these dangers impacting your life?

Beyond the reward of eternal life, what rewards might you experience in your everyday life by praying against and overcoming these dangers to your mind, body and soul?

DAY 34

CHRIST WITH ME

Christ with me

Today we come to the most famous stanza of the Breastplate Prayer. These 15 lines are often used by themselves and offer a powerful reminder of God's continual presence in our lives.

Let us take a moment to pray this segment together, slowly, line by line, breathing deeply between each line.

Christ with me,

Christ before me,

Christ behind me,

Christ in me,

Christ beneath me,

Christ above me,

Christ on my right,

Christ on my left,

Christ when I lie down,

Christ when I sit down,

Christ when I arise,

Christ in the heart of everyone who thinks of me,

Christ in the mouth of everyone who speaks of me,

Christ in every eye that sees me,

Christ in every ear that hears me.

How do you feel?

For some, this may be a comforting prayer knowing that Christ is truly present in us and around us at every turn. For others, it may be a bit unsettling. We don't mind going to God's house for a weekly visit, but do we really want God hanging out in our house? It's one thing to clean things up for an occasional guest, but we can't keep everything straight all the time. What if Jesus sees how I really live? What will he say about the mess in the house of my life?

"Christ with me…"

Honestly, this is a summary of the next 14 lines. We could simply pray, "Christ with me" and everything that follows would be implied. But there is a reason the writer broke it out in such detail. Let's take some time over the next few days to unpack each line and what it means for Christ to be present "with me".

"with" …

It's such a small and seemingly insignificant preposition, easy to read past without much thought. We see the word "with", and we immediately know there is a connection between two or more things or people. "I would like mashed potatoes with gravy" or "She is with her mom". We wouldn't bother taking time to analyze the meaning of such statements. It simply means that the two things or two people are together. We get it. Move on.

But what does it really mean for you to be "with" someone?

Am I "with" my daughter when she is watching a favorite show while I am on the couch reading? Well, yes... sort of. Are we "with" our friends when we are all sitting around the table at a restaurant on our phones, barely speaking to one another? Again, yes... sort of.

Technically we are with each other because we are "together" in the same place. If someone asked where I was, I would say I was in the living room with my daughter. If asked what we did last night, we might say we were out with friends. And these would be honest answers.

But were we really "with" them?

Physically, yes. But being together physically in the same space is not the same as being present with one another. In our world of constant distractions, being fully present in the moment is not easy. There are a million concerns that turn our thoughts away from whatever we are doing and whoever we are "with". We are not good at being present in conversations because we tend to think more about what we are going to say or do next than about what the other person is saying.

We know intellectually that Christ is with us because, as the Psalmist writes, there is nowhere we can hide from God's presence (Psalm 139:7-12). When we pray, "Christ with me," however, we must ask a deeper question:

> Do I live my life with the Holy Spirit simply hanging out in the same room or am I fully present "with" Christ who by the Spirit, chooses to be fully present "with" me?

Reflections:

Is the thought of Christ being "with you" more comforting or discomforting and why? How are your feelings different in different times, places or situations? Are there some places in your life you would rather Christ was not "with" you? When and why?

Reflect on a time when you knew God was "with you" and you were not fully present "with" God.

What steps will you take this week to be fully present "with" Christ?

DAY 35

CHRIST BEFORE ME, CHRIST BEHIND ME

> Christ before me,
> Christ behind me

Christ is with us indeed, but not as an abstract object of faith or a historical figure we learned about in Sunday School. Jesus, the Christ, is the Word Made Flesh, the Living Word of God who speaks all things into existence. The Word was there in the beginning and the Word is already present at the end of days. Christ is the Alpha and the Omega, the first and the last, the beginning and the end. Christ has been with us every step along the way and Christ has already walked the path ahead.

Christ before me.

This is what I mean when I say Christ has already walked the path ahead. This is what we mean when we say Christ is the Omega, the end, the consummation of all things. Christ before us cuts much deeper than the old cliché preachers use when they shout, "I've read the back of the book and we win!" It's not just about some final victory in heaven. Yes, Christ went to prepare a place for us in his Father's house, but Christ also goes before us here and now.

Sometimes it feels like we are playing follow the leader with Jesus through the gospels, trying desperately to keep up with all he is trying to teach us. Then we hit the beginning of Acts and whoosh, he's off in the clouds like Mary Poppins when the wind changes. How do we follow Christ up into those clouds?

Answer: We don't.

At least not yet. This is the problem we find in Acts 1:10-11. The angels find the disciples staring dumbfounded into the sky when Jesus clearly told them to go and wait in Jerusalem for the Holy Spirit's power and then to go into all the world to proclaim the Good News of God's Kingdom on earth.

This is where the "Christ behind me" part comes in. There are days when it seems like Christ has gotten just a little too far ahead. We were following along just fine and then we hit a fork in the road and we're not sure which way he turned. We choose a path and after a while we have made so many turns that we don't even know if we're still going the same direction.

Yes, Christ went to prepare a place for us and in one sense, Christ is so far ahead we cannot see the trail he has blazed. Just when it seems all hope is lost, we turn around and look back to discover that the very Christ we were chasing aimlessly through the wilderness of life is standing right behind us. We look back over our journey and realize he was with us every step of the way and we didn't even know it. Like the disciples on the road to Emmaus we ask, "Were not our hearts burning within us while he was talking to us on the road, while he was opening the scriptures to us?" (Luke 24:32). Something deep within us knew we could not possibly have been alone. Jesus would not have abandoned us. And yet we felt alone and abandoned. We didn't know which way to go and we felt lost and afraid.

Maybe you're in that place right now, feeling lost, alone and afraid. You know Christ has gone ahead of you and is calling you to something greater, but you have no idea what. This is a far more common experience than we would like. Running ahead in a state of panic rarely gets us where we need to go. It only creates more panic. Maybe we need to stop, take a breath, and turn around. We're not turning around to go back to the way things were or to wallow in the nostalgia of the good old days when everything seemed clearer. No, we're simply glancing back to get our bearings, to see where we've been and how far we've come.

And there we will see Christ, who has been right behind us the whole time, encouraging us along the way. We will realize we were never alone, and we were never really lost.

Christ before us.

Christ behind us.

It's always both. Christ is never too far away.

Reflections:

Reflect on a time when you felt lost and couldn't see the path God had for you. How did you feel and how did you respond?

Reflect on a time when you turned back to see the ways Christ had been present all along.

Where do you most need to see Christ right now, before you or behind you, and why?

DAY 36

CHRIST IN ME

Christ in me

Three simple words, and yet when it comes to the presence of Christ, this may be the most complicated line of all. We know Christ is present with us through the Holy Spirit. Let's dig deeper into this blessed mystery.

There is a reason God put on flesh and walked among us. We needed to see a God with skin. We needed a God we could identify with. We needed a God who *walks with us and talks with us and tells us we are his own.*[29]

---

[29] C. Austin Miles, "In the Garden", 1913.

If we're honest, there is a part of us that would be OK waiting for the whole "Spirit thing" until we get to heaven if we could only ask Jesus a few questions now, in person. We live in the physical world. It would be nice to talk to a physical God, even if only for a few hours or a day. As we said on Day 5 when we talked about the Ascension, Jesus in the flesh could only be in one place at a time and he could only dwell among so many people. But God desires to dwell with all people of all times. Christ sends the Spirit who does not dwell only with certain people in a certain place or certain time, but who dwells "in" every person in every place for all time.

We find ourselves with an incomprehensible mystery, for we cannot explain or conceive of a relationship that intimate. Every human relationship, no matter how close, has clear physical boundaries and personal space. For the Holy Spirit, there is no such thing as "personal space" or physical boundaries. What does it mean for a living being to dwell "in" us? It just doesn't feel right. Such intimacy may make us deeply uncomfortable. We cry out with the Psalmist, "Where can I go from your presence O God?" because part of us still lives with the shame of Eden and we do not want God to see that we are naked (Psalm 139, Genesis 3:7-11). We believe God sees everything, but we are very good at pretending to hide. Like little children, we cover our eyes and think we are invisible.

"Christ in me" can be truly freeing, if we embrace what it means to be fully known AND fully loved. This is a difficult truth to accept because we know our sin all too well. We all have things we want to hide. Perhaps this is the reason we so often live as if Christ is not present at all. "If I can't see the Holy Spirit," we reason, "maybe the Spirit can't see me." It may not be a conscious thought, but our feelings of shame before God are all too real and our futile efforts to hide only prevent us from experiencing the joy and freedom of the presence of Christ in us.

If Christ is in us, there is truly no reason to hide. Our fig leaves only keep us from knowing the love of our Father.

> My life is hidden with Christ,
> wrapped up in the covering of my Father
> My life is hidden with Christ,
> no more use in running away.
> No more use in hiding my face.
> No more use in hiding.
> There is nothing to hide.
>
> No more sons and daughters
> hiding in the closet of fear…[30]

---

[30] Andrew Ehrenzeller, *Naked*, 2011, www.andrewehrenzeller.com. Audio available at "I Arise Today – Resources," Echo, https://www.craigsefa.org/arise/resources. Day 35.

Reflections:

What first thoughts come to mind when you think about "Christ in you"?

Is the thought of God being so close and intimate comforting, frightening, or somewhere in between? Why?

How have you tried to hide from God's presence in you? Are you presently hiding and, if so, is it time to come out?

DAY 37

CHRIST BENEATH ME, CHRIST ABOVE ME

Christ beneath me,
Christ above me

Have you ever noticed where people look?

Some people seem to be staring off into space, always looking up as though lost in a daydream. Others appear downcast, often keeping their gaze toward the ground and only glancing up occasionally to speak or interact as needed.

One could make a strong argument that our instinct to

look away, either up or down, rather than maintaining eye contact with one another, says a lot about our insecurity and inability to be fully present and engaged in the moment. In general, I would agree. As a society we need to be far more intentional about being fully present with one another.

From another angle, we could use scripture to argue which is better, to look up or down.

Colossians 3:2 says to set our minds on things above and not on the things of earth. Yet some people spend so much time gazing up toward heaven, metaphorically speaking, that they end up making very little difference in the world around them. After all, they might argue, "The things of earth are passing away," so why bother with them at all (1 John 2:17, 1 Corinthians 7:31).

On the other hand, Psalm 119:105 tells us that the Word of God is a lamp unto our feet. Some recognize God's call to be good stewards of creation and to work for justice and mercy so that the Kingdom may be fulfilled "on earth as it is in heaven." Yet we can just as easily become embroiled in the despair and apparent hopelessness of the world that all our efforts to make a difference feel like an exercise in futility. Without a heavenly perspective, the world may very well consume us.

So, which is it? Do we look up to heaven, or do we focus on the path God lights up right in front of our feet?

What if it's not so absolute?

I'll leave it to the psychologists to analyze all the subconscious implications of looking up or down, but for now I would argue that, no matter our natural inclinations, God invites us to look up AND down. Keeping an eye on heaven, we find the hope we need to proclaim the Good News on earth. Keeping an eye on earth reminds us why such hope matters in the first place. Heaven is not an escape from the earth, it is the radical transformation and restoration of the earth and indeed of all creation.

If the Kingdom of God were a skyscraper, it would be built upside down. We look up to eternity to lay solid foundations that will never crumble, and we build "upside down" as it were, so the pinnacle of heaven's tower reaches all the way down to the earth where God's "penthouse suite" becomes readily accessible to all people. Like the New Jerusalem, God never shuts the gates (Revelation 21:25). The Kingdom is never out of reach, no matter how low we find ourselves in life. Jesus taught us to pray, "Thy kingdom come, thy will be done, on earth *as it is* in heaven."

Perhaps the most important thing is, no matter which direction we tend to gaze, looking in only one direction will always cause us to miss something.

Christ above us… Christ beneath us…
Christ before us… Christ behind us…

Always looking in one direction, whether up or down, will give you a kink in the neck. Maybe it's time to stretch.

Maybe Christ is saying to those who are downcast, "Hey, look, I'm UP here."

At the same time, Christ may be saying to those who are lost in the dream of heaven, "Hey, look, I'm DOWN here."

Which way is God calling you to look right now?

Whether above or beneath, Christ's invitation is the same… "Keep your eyes on me."

Reflections:

Which direction do you find yourself looking more often, up or down? Why?

Do you tend to see Christ more clearly when looking up toward heaven or when looking down at the path right in front of you? Why?

Where do you most need to see Christ in your life right now? Beneath you, guiding your steps? Or above you, giving you hope for the journey?

DAY 38

CHRIST ON MY RIGHT, CHRIST ON MY LEFT

*Christ on my right,
Christ on my left*

You must therefore be careful to do as the Lord your God has commanded you; you shall not turn to the right or to the left. You must follow exactly the path that the Lord your God has commanded you, so that you may live, and that it may go well with you, and that you may live long in the land that you are to possess (Deuteronomy 5:32-33).

Let your eyes look directly forward, and your gaze be

straight before you. Keep straight the path of your feet, and all your ways will be sure. Do not swerve to the right or to the left; turn your foot away from evil (Proverbs 4:25-27).

In these verses the Bible seems to imply that Christ is not on our right or our left... only straight ahead. To turn to the right or left is to stray into evil.

Perhaps Patrick's prayer draws more on the tradition of Job who says,

> If I go forward, he is not there; or backward, I cannot perceive him; on the left he hides, and I cannot behold him; I turn to the right, but I cannot see him. But he knows the way that I take; when he has tested me, I shall come out like gold (Job 23:8-10).

This passage recognizes that God is present with Job, before him, behind him and on his left and right. Only no matter where God may be at work, Job cannot see it.

Similarly, when Abraham separates from Lot in Genesis 13:9, Abraham gives Lot the choice whether to go right or left. For Abraham, it doesn't seem to matter which direction Lot goes. Abraham knows God will go before him and trusts God to protect his nephew as well. God's presence is not limited to one direction or another.

Finally, we come to Mark 10:35-38 where a few of the

disciples ask Jesus to sit on his right and his left in glory. Jesus says they do not understand what they are asking and makes it clear he is in no position to make such a promise. We also know that Jesus sits at the right hand of the Father. What we don't often consider is the implication that the Father sits at the "left hand" of Christ. If God the Father is on the left, the left can't be all bad.

The tradition of left and right throughout the ancient world is often divided into spiritual vs. carnal or worldly realities. In Latin, the original word for left meant "sinister." Many cultures have associated the left with "evil." Perhaps this comes from the fact that between 70 and 95% of the world's population is right-handed, leaving some throughout history to assume something is wrong with the anomalous few. Even as late as the 1950's and early 60's, my father was taught in his Catholic school that being "left-handed" was wrong and he quickly learned to be ambidextrous.

Some Christians continue this distorted use of left and right in the political realm by declaring war against the so-called evils and godlessness of the "Liberal Left" in contrast to the "Religious Right." Indeed, Biblical language is filled with examples of the left being associated with evil and sin while the right is considered righteous, but this says far more about history and culture than about reality. God did not make the "left" inferior, whether left-handed, left-brained, or left in ideology and politics.

And then of course we have those few scriptures we saw earlier that focus on avoiding both the left and the right.

It amazes me how we build entire theological systems around cultural stigmas such as the virtue or sinfulness of right and left. With God, it seems AND is almost always a better word than OR.

This idea fits nicely into my own Wesleyan tradition of the Via Media, or Middle Way in which we emphasize both head AND heart, social justice AND personal piety, etc.

Christ on the right AND Christ on the left.

What does that mean for you right now?

We all know people who are more "left" and more "right" than us and we tend to consider our own position on the spectrum superior, even if subconsciously. Some are more logical (left-brained) and some are more creative (right-brained). Some are more liberal (left) and some are more conservative (right). But what if no matter where people find themselves on all our human-conceived spectra of left and right, Christ is there… on our left, on our right, AND everywhere in between?

Reflections:

Where do you most see the issue of left vs. right show up in your life? Where do you see God on the spectrum and why?

What would it look like to see Christ on the "opposite side" from where you are standing?

If the way of God is indeed the "middle way," then Christ meets us where we are on the left and right and moves us all toward the center, toward each other, and toward our heavenly Father. How is Christ calling you toward someone else who may be coming from a very different position?

DAY 39

CHRIST WHEN I LIE DOWN
CHRIST WHEN I SIT DOWN
CHRIST WHEN I ARISE

> Christ when I lie down
> Christ when I sit down
> Christ when I arise

Much of this prayer begins with the refrain, "I arise today." It is an active prayer, seeking God's presence in every part of our day, no matter where we go and what we may experience. It is vital that when we arise, we arise with God. But there is more to life than "arising." As some have said, there are times when our "get up and go," simply "got up and went." We have nothing left. We just need to stop.

Most of the time in our culture this "stopping" comes in the form of a crash or burnout. Yellow lights mean speed up and red lights mean slam on your breaks, but there is no such thing as slowing down. Yet we acknowledge today that we not only arise with Christ, but we also sit down and lie down with Christ. Turns out that resting, or even napping, may not be a "sin" after all.

When reflecting on the poetic structure of Genesis 1, we find that on each day of creation, there was "evening and there was morning," and it was good. Perhaps the writer of St. Patrick's Prayer understood this pattern inherent within creation… evening and then morning, rest and then work, lying down, sitting up, and then arising to the day that God has already prepared for us while we were asleep.

Consider the implications of such a reversal. Rather than jumping out of bed to the obnoxious sound of an "alarm" which sends our brains into immediate alert or crisis mode, God invites us to sit up slowly and breathe in new mercies every morning. Our sense of urgency does not cause the day to begin.

The day began in the evening as we went to bed, and God has handled it quite well all night long without our help. Rather than working all day until we crash and fall into bed at night, we are invited to begin our day lying down and resting so that we might enter our work refreshed and renewed. When evening comes, we are not simply trying to unwind from the day or squeeze in a few more hours of toil. Rather, a new day has already begun, and we are invited spend the first third of this new day sitting and lying down to rest deeply in the peace of Christ.

This is not a call to be lazy. Work is as much a gift as rest. But work is not the driving force of our life. What we do when we arise does not define us. At our core, we are the same person when we arise, when we sit down and when we lie down. Christ is every bit as present in our rest as in our activity.

This is the meaning of Sabbath. The Sabbath is not something else we must fit into our schedule to please God. It is a gift from God so that we might remember who we are. Rest is God's way of reminding us we do not have to be in control 24/7. The world does not spin on our axis. While God invites us to participate in the work of caring for creation and restoring God's Kingdom on earth, that work depends far more on Christ "with us" than on what we do "for Christ."

It is easy to get fidgety and uncomfortable when we sit down or when we lie down. We feel restless, especially if circumstances such as poor health or an accident prevent us from rising and being active. Healthy or not, able or not, God invites us to rest first and then work.

Evening and then morning.

Lie down in Christ.

Sit up in Christ.

Then arise in Christ and welcome the day God has already made for you.

Reflections:

On a scale of 1 to 10, 10 being mostly refreshed and 1 being anxious and weary, how do you feel when you arise on an average morning? What factors contribute to your answer?

In what ways might your experience of God throughout the day be different if you thought of the day beginning in the evening?

How important is Sabbath in your life? Do you practice regular rhythms of rest and work? How hard is it for you to slow down? Why?

DAY 40

CHRIST IN EVERYONE

Christ in the heart of everyone who thinks of me,
Christ in the mouth of everyone who speaks of me,
Christ in every eye that sees me,
Christ in every ear that hears me

Long before I began seriously looking at this famous prayer, these lines stood out to me as among the most challenging. Christ is present everywhere and in everything, but now we pray to see Christ in everyone.

There are always great spiritual role-models in whom we clearly see the presence of Christ, but this prayer does not discriminate.

It doesn't ask us to see Christ only in spiritual giants.

It doesn't ask us to see Christ only in Christians.

It doesn't even ask us to see Christ in only "good people."

For me, these lines feel more like questions than declarations. Lord, can I really see you in everyone? Let us consider together some of the people in whom we might be asked to see the presence of Christ.

Do I feel Christ in the heart of everyone who thinks of me?

- What about those who think negatively of me?

- What about those who only think of ways to do me harm?

- What about those who think very little of me, dismissing me as though I do not matter?

- What about those who think only of how to use me or take advantage of me?

Do I hear Christ in the mouth of everyone who speaks of me?

- What about those who speak poorly of me, who spread gossip and slander my name?

- What about those who speak lies about me?

- What about those who speak behind my back?

- What about those who speak to me in hurtful or manipulative ways?

Do I see Christ in every eye that sees me?

- What about those who only see me from a distance but would never recognize me?

- What about those who only see what they want to see, but are unwilling to see the "real me"?

- What about those who only see the worst in me?

- What about those who see too much and who know me more than I want to be known?

Do I recognize Christ in every ear that hears me?

- What about those who hear only what they want to hear?

- What about those who misinterpret what they hear?

- What about those who hear, but have no interest in really listening?

- What about those who only hear what others say about me but don't really hear me?

We could go on, but I think the point is clear. There are just some people, whether we call them strangers, enemies, or something in between, who do not seem to reflect the light of Christ in their lives.

Can we really see Christ in these people?

I don't know if we can see Christ in everyone or not. For some, it will certainly be harder than others. Yet if everyone is truly created in the image of God, then don't we at least owe it to them and to ourselves to keep looking until we find even a spark of God's love which might be kindled by the power and grace of the Holy Spirit?

Jesus said that whatever we have done, or not done, unto the "least of these," we have done, or not done, for him (Matthew 25:31-46). No one in this story recognized Christ in the other, yet he was always there.

As we learn to see Christ in everyone, we must also ask one final question. How clearly can people see Christ in me?

Reflections:

Who are the people in whom I can clearly see the face of Christ and why?

Who are the people in whom I struggle to see even a glimpse of Christ's presence and why?

What will I do this week to intentionally look for Christ in someone's life where God's loving presence appears entirely absent?

DAY 41

ON ENDINGS AS NEW BEGINNINGS

> I arise today
> through a mighty strength,
> the invocation of the Trinity
> through belief in the Threeness
> through confession of the Oneness
> of the Creator of creation.
> Amen.

With this final stanza we come full circle. The end is its beginning, just as it is with our Three-One God, the Alpha and Omega, the beginning and the end.

In Biblical studies, we call such bracketing around passages of Scripture an "inclusio," which signals to the hearer that everything in between the repeated lines must be interpreted in the context of the bracket. Consider Psalm 8 as a simple illustration.

> Lord, our Lord, how majestic is your name in all the earth! (Psalm 8:1 and Psalm 8:9, NIV).

Everything in between these verses unpacks the nature of God's majesty from the perspective of the Psalmist. And so it is with our prayer. Everything we have prayed throughout this 40-day journey begins and ends with the Three-One God, the Creator of Creation. It is only through the mighty strength of our Creator that we can arise at all, let alone arise in or summon the many ways that strength manifests itself in our everyday lives. While the rest of the prayer shows us the characteristics of Christ's strong presence in and with and through us, the beginning and the end point us back to the source.

As we noted on day 11, the distinctiveness of the Celtic Cross is found in the addition of a circle at its center. In countless spiritual traditions, including the paganism of the Celtic people prior to the arrival of Christianity, the circle stands as a primary symbol reminding us of the sun's central role in sustaining life on earth.

The circle also draws our attention to eternity, a reality which has no beginning and no end, and it reminds us that all life is connected in this infinite circle throughout time and space.

The "circle" of St. Patrick's Breastplate prayer reminds us that the circle which binds all life together in eternity is not some mystical or metaphysical phenomenon. It is not a life-force flowing out of creation. It is the eternal circle of the Three-One God, Father, Son and Holy Spirit. The Father eternally speaks the Word into being and the Word eternally sends forth the Holy Spirit by which all things and all persons are created.

As our journey through this prayer comes to an end, may it also be a new beginning. May you arise each day through the mighty strength of the "eternal circle", God, the giver and sustainer of life, whose mercies are new every morning and whose love and faithfulness, like the circle, knows no end.

> In our end is our beginning;
>   in our time, infinity;
> In our doubt there is believing;
>   in our life, eternity,
> In our death, a resurrection;
>   at the last, a victory,
> Unrevealed until its season,
>   something God alone can see.[31]

---

[31] Natalie Sleeth, "Hymn of Promise" (Hope Publishing Co., 1986).

Reflections:

As the end of this journey calls you back to the beginning, reflect on how this prayer has shaped and influenced your experience of Christ's presence in your everyday life.

How might the eternal circle at the center of the cross impact the way you understand the meaning and scope of Christ's sacrifice?

"In the end is our beginning." As your journey through this prayer comes to an end, to what new beginning do you sense God calling you?

MAY THE ROAD RISE UP TO MEET YOU

May the road rise up to meet you.

May the wind be always at your back.

May the sun shine warm upon your face;

the rains fall soft upon your fields

and until we meet again,

may God hold you in the palm of His hand.

(traditional gaelic blessing)

ABOUT THE AUTHOR

Craig J. Sefa serves as an Ordained Elder in the Western North Carolina Conference of the United Methodist Church.

Craig is a graduate of Duke Divinity School with a Doctor of Ministry and Asbury Theological Seminary with a Master of Divinity and a Master of Arts in Theological Studies.

Craig is a husband, father, pastor, teacher, writer and musician with a passion for Spiritual Formation and Discipleship. He is also an active participant and board member of the Wesleyan Contemplative Order (wesleyancontemplativeorder.com).

Visit Craig's website and blog at:

craigsefa.org
"echoing the whispers of heaven"

Printed in Great Britain
by Amazon